Louisiana Architecture
A Handbook on Styles

Louisiana Architecture
A Handbook on Styles

by
Jonathan Fricker
Donna Fricker
Patricia L. Duncan

photography by
Donna Fricker

Published by
The Center for Louisiana Studies
University of Southwestern Louisiana
Lafayette, Louisiana

Front Cover Image:
Poplar Grove, West Baton Rouge Parish, 1884.
Photograph by Donna Fricker.

Library of Congress Number: 98-71639
ISBN Number: 1-887366-23-7

Published by The Center for Louisiana Studies
P.O. Box 40831
University of Southwestern Louisiana
Lafayette, LA 70504-0831

Contents

Acknowledgments

This volume describing and illustrating the architectural styles found in Louisiana would not have been possible without the help of several organizations. The authors wish to thank the Louisiana Department of Culture, Recreation and Tourism, whose Office of Cultural Development, Division of Historic Preservation provided the time and opportunity needed to photograph, study and interpret the state's architectural legacy. We also wish to recognize the Office of the Lieutenant Governor, whose goal of promoting the best that is Louisiana is the underlying reason behind all our work.

In addition, we wish to thank the Preservation Resource Center of New Orleans for its constant support of the project. The style articles originally appeared in *Preservation In Print,* a publication produced jointly by the PRC and the Division of Historic Preservation. PRC staff members were among the first to suggest that the material be republished in a single volume for use by the general public. The generosity of the organization's Board of Directors in granting permission to reprint the essays is deeply appreciated.

Finally, we wish to thank the Center for Louisiana Studies, University of Southwestern Louisiana for its recognition of the topic's importance and its enthusiasm for the project.

J. F.
D. F.
P. L. D.

Preface

Back in the 1950s, when machine technology and modern architecture were still going to save the world, a curious thing happened. Public and academic disgust with the "dour" and "frightful" buildings of the Victorian age began to abate. As interest grew, people were perplexed, for they did not know what to make of these curious relics with their wild skylines, decoratively shingled walls, curlicue brackets and knobby columns. But now, after a generation or so of study, the popular styles that graced the American buildingscape during the nineteenth and early twentieth centuries are fairly well known to preservationists. Much of this was set forth in 1969 in Marcus Whiffen's pioneering work, *American Architecture since 1780: A Guide to the Styles.*

Whiffen, as it is known, has become a major handbook for field preservationists, and since that time, other guides have appeared. But these have not always been very useful in Louisiana, simply because our state is so different from the national norm. There are some American styles that virtually never appeared in Louisiana. Gothic and Tuscan villas and cottages of the likes of Andrew Jackson Downing come to mind. They were a national craze of the early Victorian era, but in Louisiana one can count the examples literally on one hand. Add to this the Parisian Second Empire style, with its generous and often bulbous mansard roofs. This gouty scion of the great "Gilded Age" made little impact here despite its French provenance. Then, too, styles that did become popular in our state often had Louisiana permutations quite unlike the national norms. Then there is that glory of our heritage, the French Creole tradition, which, with minor exceptions, appears in no other state.

The need for a clear statement on Louisiana styles has long been recognized. The essays that follow first appeared as a series in *Preservation In Print* which ran in 1993 and 1994. This publication is a joint project of the Preservation Resource Center of New Orleans and the Louisiana Division of Historic Preservation, Office of Cultural Development, Department of Culture, Recreation and Tourism. The authors, as members of the Division's staff, have at present a total of 47 years experience in examining Louisiana's historic buildings. Many of the observations contained in these essays uniquely reflect that experience.

In this we have come to know and savor the richness of our architectural heritage. All in all, one could hardly spend a career in a more delightful pursuit.

Jonathan Fricker, Director
Division of Historic Preservation
Baton Rouge
January 1998

Louisiana Architecture
A Handbook on Styles

The French Creole Style

by Patricia L. Duncan

When most people think of Louisiana, they concentrate on the food, the French language, and the zest with which Louisianians celebrate life. Nevertheless, preservationists would suggest that the state's French Creole architecture plays an equally important role in making Louisiana unique. The French attempted to colonize a vast area along the Gulf Coast and up the Mississippi River into America's heartland. However, their settlements were thinly scattered, and they were eventually overwhelmed by the expanding American republic. Although a few historic French buildings can be found outside Louisiana, only in the southern and central sections of the state do remnants of French culture and language, and a significantly large collection of French Creole buildings, survive. However, the tradition is only now beginning to receive the appreciation it deserves. Creole architecture may be the only one of America's three major colonial building traditions to have at least partially evolved in the New World. The British and Spanish, as well as lesser colonial powers such as the Flemish, Dutch, and Swedes, completely imported building types from home rather than developing new building forms.

Just who were these people who contributed so much to the state's cultural milieu? The word "Creole" itself is confusing because its meaning has changed over time. Adapted from the Spanish word *criollo*, it originally referred to white children born in the Caribbean. In Louisiana, people of European descent, and especially the descendants of French settlers, were called Creoles. Later, the term was also used to denote Louisiana's large population of persons of mixed European and African descent. It is the concept of mixture which best defines the word "Creole" today and, in fact, best defines Creole architecture.

Louisiana's eighteenth- and nineteenth-century Creoles were a permissive, fun-loving, and status-conscious people with a fondness for European courtly customs. These included good manners, lavish hospitality, close family ties, dancing, and gambling. Creoles also practiced the widespread European custom of dueling—over both important and trivial matters. In addition, they sanctioned a double moral standard which placed women on pedestals but encouraged young men to sow their wild oats.

The Creoles left Louisiana two very different types of dwellings. The first is the Creole cottage, which they built in both rural and urban locations. The second is the urban Creole townhouse, which is found in large numbers in New Orleans and, to a much lesser extent, in Natchitoches. In addition to dwellings, the Creole building tradition spawned an important outbuilding type, the *pigeonnier.*

Creole cottages can be defined by the features they shared. Heavy braced timber frames and Norman truss roof systems formed the structure, with bricks or a confection of mud and Spanish moss called *bousillage* filling the space between the timbers. Houses were raised several feet off the ground on piers or blocks. The earliest Creole houses had broken pitch roofs. Later, straightly pitched gable or hipped roofs were preferred in both urban and rural areas. Despite the large attic space available beneath the high rooflines, the Creoles almost never utilized the attic for daily living. Most Creole houses had generous galleries set beneath their broad, spreading rooflines. Depending upon the weather, the gallery might serve as a sitting or dining room, with curtains hung from iron rods between the columns to provide shade. Thus, the Creoles decorated their galleries as outdoor rooms with chair rails, wainscoting, and cornices. Multiple French doors opened from the gallery into the rooms. Urban cottages displayed similar floor plans and decorative elements but usually lacked the commodious galleries found on rural

Baton Rouge's Joseph Petitpierre House is a finely crafted example of a small Creole cottage. Restored in the late 1980s, it won the Grand Prize in the National Trust for Historic Preservation's 1989 Great American Home Awards Competition. Photo by Donna Fricker.

examples. Instead, the house stood flush with the property line or adjacent side-walk. The latter was protected from the elements by a change in roofline pitch, known today as a "kick," which extended the roof outward.

The floor plans of Creole houses varied greatly in size. The plan always con-sisted of at least one range of rooms typically paralleled by a front gallery. This range included a nearly square *salle* (parlor), with at least one narrow *chambre* (bed-room) located next to it. Larger houses had from three to five rooms across the front. Sometimes, a second range of rooms stood behind the first. Most Creole houses had a rear *cabinet*/loggia range (a central open area flanked by a room at each corner) as well. The houses usually lacked hallways; instead, the rooms opened directly into each other. Decorative elements preferred by the Creoles included turned or chamfered gallery columns, exposed beaded ceiling beams, the use of a French diamond shaped parallelogram called a lozenge, and wraparound mantels. The latter centered upon boxed chimney flues located on interior walls. Elegant overmantels were found in the wealthier homes.

As colonial planters prospered, they began building grander cottages. The raised Creole plantation house featured most of the distinguishing traits found in

The facade of this New Orleans cottage illustrates the Creoles' general lack of concern for symmetry. Only after southern and central Louisiana began filling with Anglo-Americans, who brought with them their own architectural traditions, did the facades of Creole houses become symmetrical. Photo by Donna Fricker.

A larger Creole dwelling, Little Texas in St. James Parish has two full ranges of rooms. The Greek Revival transom and sidelights outlining the home's central entrance illustrate how the Creoles adapted Anglo-American architectural ideas without sacrificing the essence of the Creole style. Photo by Jay Edwards.

Wraparound mantels with elegant overmantels characterized high style Creole taste. This mantel is one of three within the Jones House in Natchitoches Parish. Photo by Donna Fricker.

Homeplace is a raised Creole plantation house in St. Charles Parish. The finest house type built by French Louisianians, these homes were once quite common in rural areas. Now only about thirty are known to survive in the entire state. Photo by Patricia L. Duncan.

the single story cottage but had additional special characteristics. Homeplace, on the west bank of the Mississippi River near Hahnville, is such a house. Although in some raised plantation houses a dining room was included on the lower floor, the ground floor at Homeplace consists of an unfinished above-ground brick basement story used for storage and other utilitarian purposes. Its highly decorated frame upper floor serves as the primary living space. The house has a fully encircling gallery on both levels. A row of thick brick columns outlines the lower gallery, while narrow turned columns outline the upper. Stairways connecting the two floors are located on the exterior. The raised Creole plantation house was the absolute apex of Creole architecture in Louisiana.

Louisiana's Acadian settlers also built a version of the Creole cottage. The Acadians were descendants of French peasant settlers from Nova Scotia who arrived in Louisiana between 1765 and 1790. The Acadian cottage generally featured a two-room-wide plan, with a gallery across the facade and a *cabinet*/loggia range at the rear. Unlike the Creoles, who expanded this basic house type into the larger structures described above, the Acadians never expanded the type beyond this small configuration. In addition, they imported certain building preferences which

The *pigeonnier* at Magnolia Plantation in Natchitoches Parish. One wonders if these ornamental towers are related to the towers on late medieval castles and manor houses. Photo by
Donna Fricker.

distinguished their homes from those of the Creoles. These included the custom of using attics as living spaces and the resulting need to provide a staircase or ladder to reach this area. East of the Atchafalaya Basin these stairs usually appeared on the rear loggia or in a *cabinet*. West of the basin, narrow, steep staircases were located on the front gallery.[1] Today these houses can still be found throughout the region of Louisiana known as Acadiana.

Pigeonniers, small towers with nesting boxes for birds on their upper floors, were found on the most prosperous of Creole plantations. Frequently the lower story contained an office or *garçonnière* (young man's apartment). *Pigeonniers* usually came in pairs and were placed so as to ornament the overall appearance of the plantation complex. Today there are less than twenty of these important structures left in the entire state.

Experts disagree on the origin of the Creole cottage, with some scholars variously claiming its important features to be imported from France, Canada, and the West Indian islands colonized by the French. Others emphasize the importance which accommodating Louisiana's damp ground and humid climate played in developing the style.[2] The most likely case is that the Creole house resulted from a combination of imported ideas and local needs.

One theory focuses upon the Italian double-loggia house as the inspiration for the Creole cottage.[3] This house type had appeared in the West Indies by the sixteenth century. According to this idea, there its front loggia was replaced by a full length gallery, but its rear loggia and flanking rooms remained intact. The Creoles came to call these rear corner rooms *cabinets*. Frenchmen settling in the Caribbean may have copied this house but changed the internal plan to reflect their preference for asymmetrical room arrangements. Whatever its origin, the theory argues, it was this adapted house which French West Indian planters brought to Louisiana. There it blended with the Canadian spreading roof and internal chimney, the French wraparound mantel, and a particular type of timber frame construction native to the farmhouses of northern France. Of course, the new Louisiana house was a vernacular adaptation using local materials such as *bousillage*.

The Creole townhouse was a multi-story, timber frame and masonry structure in which the main block stood flush to the sidewalk. Its dependencies were usually attached to one side of the structure, resulting in an "L" shaped building. The townhouse had either party walls or only a narrow passage between each house and its neighbor. Its first floor served as mercantile space and its upper floors served as the family's primary living area. Some had a low mezzanine-type storage area known as an *entresol* located between the first and second floor. The *entresol* was lighted by semicircular grilles or fanlights placed above first floor entrances. The family's area featured French doors, wooden or iron balconies cantilevered above the front sidewalk, and rear galleries providing additional outdoor living space. A wide, gated carriage passage known as a *porte-cochère* connected the street to a rear courtyard. Contrary to popular belief, townhouse courtyards were not used as gardens before 1865, and the lushly planted courtyards known today did not develop until the early years of the twentieth century.[4]   Instead, courtyards were utilitarian spaces surrounded by service structures such as stables, kitchens, wash buildings, privies, *garçonnières,* and slave quarters. In Natchitoches, an excellent example of the Creole townhouse is the building known as Ducournau Square.

The inspiration for Creole townhouses is just as unclear as that of the Creole cottage. At least two theories attempting to account for the townhouse's development have emerged. One hypothesis credits the townhouse to the influence of Spanish officials who controlled most of present-day Louisiana from 1762 to 1800. Another finds prototypes for the Creole townhouse in France.

The Spanish theory is based largely upon the fact that the townhouse did not appear in New Orleans until after fires in 1788 and 1794 destroyed much of the city. Thus, it was Spanish officials who controlled all building regulations at the time of

With living quarters located above commercial space, townhouses like Natchitoches' Ducournau Square were practical homes for Creoles living in crowded urban areas. However, the plan of this townhouse differs from the norm because its dependencies are arranged around its courtyard, making a "U" rather than an "L" shaped building. Photo by Donna Fricker.

reconstruction. In addition, many were constructed for prominent Spaniards. The Hispanic influence can supposedly be seen in the barrel tile roofing, paving tiles, wrought-iron balustrade work and flat or almost flat rooflines which appeared on buildings during this period. Perhaps the best known champion of the Spanish theory was the noted New Orleans architect and architectural historian Samuel Wilson.[5]

The French theory suggests that Creole townhouses were modeled after dwellings found in prosperous eighteenth-century Parisian neighborhoods. These homes, in turn, had been inspired by a type of closed-court farmstead which can still be seen in northern France. According to this theory, the general plan of the Creole townhouse closely matches the arrangement of these three-part Parisian houses. The first section of the French prototype was a main block of two or more stories. The second portion was a series of narrow, shed-roofed service buildings separated from the main block by a set of winder stairs. The third part of the dwelling was a private courtyard garden surrounded on all sides by the previously mentioned buildings or tall masonry walls. This garden was connected to the street by a *porte-cochère*. Some of these houses even featured French doors and open galleries facing the courtyard. Louisiana State University cultural geographer Jay Edwards introduced the French theory for the origin of the Creole townhouse in a 1993 journal article.[6] In the end, the reader must draw his or her own conclusions concerning the possible inspirations for the Creole cottage and townhouse.

Whatever its origins, the Creole building tradition dominated the state well into the nineteenth century. Although the houses changed slightly as the Creoles observed new architectural trends brought by Americans, Creole houses were built well into the 1880s. Some experts would argue that they were built even later, and in truth, modern houses with Creole rooflines and galleries can be seen in late twentieth-century suburbs throughout southern Louisiana.

The Greek Revival Style

by Jonathan Fricker

Some of the most interesting literature concerning the Greek Revival was written by its detractors. Andrew Jackson Downing, an advocate of "carpenter Gothic," decried what he termed the "tasteless temples" of the Grecian style. To him, "a dwelling house should look like a dwelling house," and a house designed to resemble a Greek temple was an aesthetic and moral lie.[1] This was the Victorian view. To a later generation of Americans, the Greek Revival represented our nation's eager and searching adolescence—a young democracy yearning for identity. It was truly a national style that swept all before it. And whatever its merits, the Greek Revival was pivotal to the South, providing Southerners an enduring architectural symbol, the white-columned mansion.

A fifth century B.C. Greek temple at Paestum in southern Italy.
Courtesy Michael Desmond.

Greek temple garden folly designed by James "Athenian" Stuart at Shugborough Estate in Staffordshire, England. Constructed just prior to the American Revolution, this is thought to be one of the first Greek Revival buildings in the world. Photo by Donna Fricker.

Surprisingly, Greek architecture was not discovered until comparatively late. Although the Renaissance in its various phases had sought for centuries to emulate the architecture and civilization of ancient Rome, Greek architecture (as apart from Roman) only became known in the West about 1760. James Stuart, a British architect, made a pilgrimage to Greece with Nicholas Revett in 1751. Stuart and Revett subsequently published *Antiquities of Athens,* a multi-volume work which had little immediate impact. "Athenian Stuart," as he was sometimes styled, designed a few small buildings in the Grecian taste. He never received many commissions and finally died in obscurity in 1788.[2] Being perhaps the father of the Greek Revival is his one footnote in history.

Brought up on Roman forms, architects first dismissed the ancient Greek style as too primitive. But increasingly its gravity and simplicity began to be admired. It dovetailed well with the rationalist, stripped-down school of classicism that prevailed among advanced architects around the turn of the nineteenth century. In Britain the Greek Revival culminated in the 1820s and 1830s, competing mainly with Gothic as the preferred style for churches and gentlemen's residences. Indeed, the architectural practice of the day can be summed up as a contest between the Greeks and the Goths. Ultimately, the Goths won.[3]

Madewood, 1840-48, Assumption Parish, Henry Howard, architect.
Photo courtesy State Office of Tourism.

Brame-Bennett House, c. 1840, Clinton. Photo by Donna Fricker.

But this was not the case in America where the Greek Revival attained a nationwide popularity it enjoyed nowhere else. Indeed, it has been said that in America "the country was studded with 'temples' from courthouses down to bird boxes."[4] The reasons for this are various. There was the Greek war for independence from Turkey in the 1820s which became a *cause célèbre.* There was also a tendency in the young republic to identify with the Greek democracies of old, as was seen not only in Greek buildings, but in new towns with Greek names on the expanding western frontier. Names spring to mind such as Ithaca, New York; Demopolis, Alabama; and Athens and Homer, Louisiana.

The rage for Greek culture may have climaxed in 1832 when Congress commissioned the eminent sculptor Horatio Greenough to create a monumental statue of George Washington. In the executed work, the father of our country is not the tall distinguished figure in colonial garb we remember; rather he is a muscular colossus sporting the flowing robes of a Greek god.[5]

A final reason for the Greek Revival's popularity is that for a long time there was no serious competition from other historic styles. As Nicholas Biddle, longtime political foe of President Andrew Jackson, wrote: "The two great truths in the world are the Bible and Grecian architecture."[6]

In the South, Grecian architecture appeared in various forms, some of which differed significantly from the national norm. In its purest form, the Greek Revival attempted to mimic the look of real Greek temples, with a huge pedimented portico spanning the entire front of a building. Such buildings featured massive round columns more or less correctly styled to the various Greek orders. Relatively heavy and blocky, temple houses such as Madewood near Napoleonville feature rich details such as Greek scroll volutes atop the columns. Of course, one has to allow that real Greek temples did not have windows or balconies. Nonetheless, Madewood's Grecian effect is pronounced and striking. A superb smaller example is the beautifully detailed Brame-Bennett House in Clinton. The temple form is also found in Louisiana in various non-residential forms, ranging from grand Gallier Hall in New Orleans to a country store in Keatchie. An adaptation of the classical temple form was a pedimented portico attached to a larger building.

Although the temple was the most popular form for houses and other buildings in the United States as a whole, it was not as common in Louisiana. Here the local French Creole style evolved over about fifty years into what became a distinctive Southern subspecies of the Greek Revival. Known to architectural historians as the "peripteral mode," it consists of a squarish house surrounded by massive columns and lacking porticoes. Columns are usually surmounted by a heavy horizontal member known as an entablature. Peripteral plantation houses include Houmas House, Ashland-Belle Hélène, Oak Alley, and the Hermitage, all on the River Road. Two courthouses in the style are the East Feliciana Parish Courthouse in Clinton and the Claiborne Parish Courthouse in Homer.

Keatchie Store, c. 1850, DeSoto Parish.
Photo by Jim Zietz.

In Louisiana, as in other states, Greek Revival buildings are marked by the use of square head openings both for windows and doors. There were no round or elliptical arches, that is unless the architect erred. The keystone arch, which made round-head openings and archways possible, was a Roman invention and was unknown to the earlier Greek civilization. Hence true Grecian style buildings do not have them.

Often builders would simplify buildings by, for example, omitting the reed-like fluting from the shafts of Ionic columns or by substituting a plain molded column capital for an authentic Grecian one. A very common treatment was to substitute plain square pillars for round columns. This still provided a Grecian look but at lesser expense. It was also better suited to wood construction, which, of course, was the overwhelming choice of Greek Revival builders and architects, especially in Louisiana. (Real Greek temples were of marble.) Interestingly enough, the white-column look, so prized in the Greek Revival South, was in fact an architectural mistake. Real Greek temples were painted red, yellow, and blue. But by the eighteenth century the paint had long since faded away, revealing the white marble underneath. When at last these temples were discovered, their white appearance was taken for an authentic Grecian look.

Houmas House, Ascension Parish, 1840. Photo courtesy State Office of Tourism.

By the 1840s, white columns or simplified square pillars were becoming commonplace in Louisiana. There were many buildings that made no pretense of being Greek in shape or form but which adopted Grecian details. For example, when the standard Louisiana Creole galleried cottage was fitted with substantial square pillars and a heavy entablature it became Greek, at least in spirit. Such a house might also have Grecian pediment-shaped tops on the windows and mantels with a heavy entablature on pillars. This type of residence became the standard for small to medium-sized plantation houses as well as for town residences on large lots. In the cities Greek details were applied to the standard three-story brick row house. Many fine examples still stand in the New Orleans Central Business District.

In much of America the Greek Revival gave way to other styles in the decade or so prior to the Civil War. But in Louisiana the style was remarkably tenacious, with full-blown examples from the 1870s and even later. Emilie Plantation House near Garyville is a case in point. It looks for all the world like a handsome substantial Greek Revival house built circa 1850. However, it dates from 1882. The moldings and corner fireplaces built for burning coal give it away. This not so ancient piece of Grecian architecture speaks volumes for the state's architectural conservatism.

Louisiana is one of a limited number of states where the Greek Revival exhibited its most spectacular flowering. Fortunately, some of these jewels are open to the public, providing an excellent opportunity to study first-hand the style that swept America.

Above: The Oaks, c. 1855, De Soto Parish. Photo by Donna Fricker.
Below: Anthemions accenting the great central doorway at Bocage, c. 1840,
Ascension Parish. These stylized plant forms were a popular decorative device
on Greek temples. Photo by Donna Fricker.

A detail from the Doric frieze at the Brame-Bennett House, Clinton. The narrow vertical three-part elements are called triglyphs, the plain spaces between are metopes, and the decorative blocks above are known as mutules. Photo by Donna Fricker.

Grecian doorway at Brame-Bennett House, Clinton. Note the upper member which protrudes beyond the frame. This decorative device is known as shoulder or ear molding. Note also the slightly pointed top suggesting a Grecian pediment. Photo by Donna Fricker.

The Gothic Revival Style

by Donna Fricker

Regarded by its proponents as "truthful" and inherently Christian, the Gothic Revival emerged in America during the 1840s as an alternative to the Greek Revival. To those unconcerned about its moral implications, the style conjured up romantic images of medieval England. Indeed, in disparaging one "sham" Gothic castle, the Louisiana Statehouse, Mark Twain blamed Sir Walter Scott, who had "run the people mad" with his "medieval romances."[1]

Like the Greek Revival, the Gothic Revival was embraced for a wide range of buildings, from churches, to residences, to schools, to prisons. There was even a Gothic doghouse built in Maine![2] A notable deviance in Louisiana from the national norm was the unpopularity of the style for residences. Like Southerners on the whole, Louisianians clung tenaciously to the beloved white-columned Greek Revival.

Of course, any analysis of the Gothic Revival must begin in the country of its origin. England turned to its Gothic past with renewed interest in the mid-eighteenth century. At first the style was not a serious one, being confined largely to garden pavilions and an appreciation of ruins. Indeed, if a gentleman did not have a genuine Gothic ruin on his estate, he could construct one, complete with hastily planted ivy and overgrowth—in short, instant antiquity. It was Strawberry Hill, the Gothic fantasy house of wealthy and influential Horace Walpole, that gave the style social standing. By the turn of the nineteenth century it was one of various exotic styles fashionable for a gentleman's residence.[3]

In the 1830s the Gothic Revival in England came to be looked on "not as a style, but as a religion," observed Kenneth Clark. This moral phase provided the enduring notion that Gothic is a Christian style *per se*, and as such, is singularly appropriate for churches. This idea was part of an overall reform effort in the Anglican church known as the ecclesiological movement. Ecclesiologists looked to the Middle Ages as a sublime period in the nation's history. It was the Age of Faith when devout and good people built "good buildings." Hence, these "good buildings" (medieval Gothic churches) were by definition Christian. As one proponent explained: "A Gothic Church, in its perfection, is an exposition of the distinctive doctrines of Christianity, clothed upon with a material form. . . ." In an 1839 statement of purpose the ecclesiologists noted that Gothic was indeed the only Christian style.[4]

A principal goal of the ecclesiologists was to encourage the study and preservation of England's medieval churches and to promote them as models for new

St. Stephen's Episcopal Church (1850s), Innis vicinity, Pointe Coupée Parish.
Photo by Donna Fricker.

churches. And not just any Gothic church should be the inspiration. Ecclesiologists specifically advanced parish churches from the Early English and Decorated phases of the Gothic as the most appropriate (thirteenth and fourteenth centuries). The last phase, the Perpendicular, was over-ornamented and hence decadent. Very importantly, the ecclesiologists insisted upon historical accuracy in neo-Gothic church construction. They were also architectural missionaries in the sense that a major goal was to spread the word to what they termed "the colonies." In 1847, a separate but parallel organization was founded in America, the New York Ecclesiological Society.[5] In England the movement was tied to the Anglican church, and in America to its counterpart, the Episcopal church.

Louisiana has two churches directly influenced by the ecclesiological movement: Christ Church in Napoleonville and St. Stephen's in Pointe Coupée Parish. Both were built in the 1850s from designs supplied by Frank Wills, the official architect of the New York Ecclesiological Society.

St. Stephen's is a good case study of the fundamental elements of a Gothic Revival church. The overall emphasis is upon verticality, a hallmark of the style. Like its medieval prototypes, the nave (main worship space) and chancel (altar area) are clearly differentiated on the exterior. Windows and other openings take the form of a pointed arch, the feature most closely associated with the style. Piers

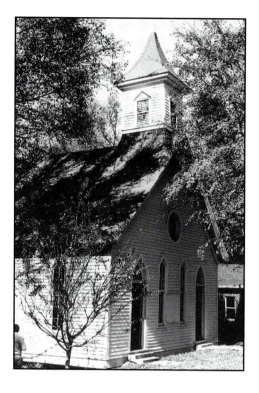

Robeline Methodist Church (1883), Natchitoches Parish, a good example of the type of simple Gothic Revival frame church found in Louisiana. Photo by Donna Fricker.

called buttresses provide structural support. A handsome three-stage entrance tower culminates in projections (in this case, of a simple pointed variety) called pinnacles. The tower is finished along the top edges with indentations known as crenelation or battlements. Originally battlements were placed atop castle walls for defensive purposes; later in the Middle Ages the device became purely decorative. In the Gothic Revival battlements were found on everything from churches to houses to state capitols.

Of course, other Gothic Revival churches built throughout Louisiana by various denominations represent the ecclesiological movement in its largest sense. As its proponents wished, Gothic was the style that immediately came to mind when thinking of building a new church. In short, it was the Christian style, a thought that is still with us today, with the mere sight of a pointed-arch window conjuring up heavenly images.

The Gothic Revival remained a popular design choice for churches in Louisiana well into the twentieth century, in one form or another. Most examples are of wood construction, reflecting a distinctly American phenomenon known as "carpenter Gothic."

An excellent example is Grace Memorial Episcopal Church in Hammond, built in 1876. Striking verticality is achieved through a bell tower with a soaring spire and the use of board-and-batten siding culminating in miniature pointed arches.

Grace Memorial Episcopal Church, 1876, Hammond. Photo by Donna Fricker.

Above: Old State Capitol, Baton Rouge, 1847-52, James Dakin, Architect. Below: One of two huge crenelated octagonal towers on the river elevation of the Old State Capitol.
Photos by Donna Fricker.

Other Gothic features, besides the signature pointed-arch openings, are pinnacles defining the edges and a trefoil design in the front gable. Sadly, the church has lost one of its most delightful Gothic features, an elaborate bargeboard of small arches accenting the front gable and the tower's gabled projections. Also, originally the front gable and second stage of the tower were covered with shingles instead of the present clapboards.

As has been mentioned, churches certainly did not have a corner on the Gothic Revival market, although they are the most numerous in Louisiana. The state's most famous example of the style is the Old State Capitol, Mark

Twain's "sham castle," built between 1847 and 1852. Dramatically sited on high ground on the banks of the Mississippi, the old statehouse is a virtuoso performance by James H. Dakin. The style chosen by the architect is termed "castellated Gothic" because of its obvious parallels with a feudal castle. On the river elevation ninety-foot crenelated octagonal towers flank a massive pointed-arch window filled with stained glass. Pointed arches and quatrefoils are everywhere one looks. What a vision this must have been to steamboat travelers. The interior of the old statehouse is also Gothic Revival, dating from William A. Freret's early 1880s "restoration" of the building, which had been gutted by fire during the Civil War.

The Old State Capitol is the only surviving institutional example of the Gothic Revival in Louisiana. Three other large castellated examples are long gone: the United States Marine Hospital, 1838-49, located near New Orleans; the Asylum for the Deaf and Dumb in Baton Rouge, 1852; and a railroad station (1851) in Carrollton, once a separate city but now a part of New Orleans.[6]

As alluded to earlier, Gothic Revival residences in Louisiana are a rarity. Andrew Jackson Downing, the extremely influential landscape architect turned architectural theorist who directed American taste toward Gothic "cottages," had little influence in the state. Seeking to promote a type of house in harmony with its setting, Downing felt that the "tasteless temples" of the Greek Revival were deceitful when used for domestic architecture. "A dwelling house should look like a dwelling house," he wrote.[7] His immensely popular books *Cottage Residences* (1842) and *The Architecture of Country Houses* (1850) were replete with drawings of recommended designs that he felt were more "truthful." While many of the designs reflect other styles, Downing's preference was for Gothic, and his name has become synonymous with the style in its domestic form.

There were only a handful of Gothic residences ever built in Louisiana. Some, like the Wilkinson House in New Orleans, are similar to the Gothic cottages advocated by Downing, while others are traditional houses with applied Gothic detailing, usually on the gallery. The state's most extravagant Gothic residence, Afton Villa in West Feliciana Parish, burned in 1963. A late example of the style is the striking Ardoyne Plantation House in Terrebonne Parish, built c. 1894.

The Gothic Revival was also a popular choice for above-ground tombs in New Orleans, which is entirely appropriate given its Christian overtones. Metairie Cemetery, founded in 1872, is an excellent place to view late nineteenth-century examples of the style. Because large, elaborate above-ground tombs reached their zenith at this time, Metairie has various spectacular examples as well as a Gothic receiving chapel. The very grandest tombs are in effect small Gothic chapels, complete with buttresses and spires thrusting heavenward. The most unusual is the Egan tomb, built in the form of a ruined Gothic chapel.

This young ancient ruin brings us full circle to the beginnings of the Gothic Revival in England. While enthusiasm for what has been called "the pointed style" was not as fervent in Louisiana as in the Northeast, it nonetheless produced many extraordinary buildings, some of which have been lost. The delightful examples that remain remind us of a style with a profoundly moral foundation—a style that to Downing was "truthful" and to the ecclesiologists was inherently Christian.

Above: The distinguishing features of a Gothic Revival residence can be seen at the Wilkinson House in New Orleans (1849), including prominent, steeply pitched gables with Gothic motifs such as trefoils and quatrefoils cut into the bargeboards, hood molds over the windows, decorative braces on the porch suggestive of pointed arches, and stylized trefoil and quatrefoil designs in the porch balustrades. Photo by Donna Fricker.

Left: Trefoil ornamentation on the bargeboards of the Wilkinson House. The cutout design at the very edge is a quatrefoil, featuring four arcs in its design. Photo by Donna Fricker.

Ardoyne, c. 1894, Terrebonne Parish, W. C. Williams & Brother, Architects.
Photo by Donna Fricker.

The late nineteenth-century Egan tomb in Metairie Cemetery, New Orleans.
Photo by Donna Fricker.

The Italianate Style

by Jonathan Fricker

If the high church Gothic Revival was the architecture of righteousness, its contemporary, the Italianate style, was the architecture of conspicuous consumption. It was a romantic style based rather loosely upon Italian villas and palazzi and the architecture of the Renaissance. Fanciful and lavish, the Italianate style provided a growing Victorian middle class with a means to express its newfound wealth. By the eve of the Civil War, it had supplanted the more sober Greek Revival, providing Louisiana a whole new set of rich and interesting archetypes. The Italianate style reached Louisiana in about 1850 and remained popular for large houses into the 1880s. For smaller builder-designed houses and commercial buildings it continued somewhat later.

Italy has long been regarded as a place of great art and civilization. It was the place of the "grand tour" in which aristocratic young men could begin to cultivate their taste. In the romantic vision of early nineteenth-century England, Italy was also a sunny and exotic place, far more attractive than the mists of the north. The Italian style was popularized in numerous European publications, and by the 1820s had achieved a modest following in England. During those years it was one of a number of styles of choice for country villas, townhouses, and commercial buildings.

Andrew Jackson Downing's enormously popular pattern books popularized the Italianate style in America just as they had the Gothic Revival. Downing recommended the style for warm climates such as the Southern states.[1] In her dissertation on the Italianate in New Orleans, Joan Caldwell notes that acceptance of the style in America coincided with a shift in attitudes toward art and luxury.[2] To Americans of the early nineteenth century, art and ornament were wasteful extravagances. J. T. Headley, an American visitor to Naples, is a case in point. After viewing the splendors of the five palaces owned by the King of Naples, and contrasting them with the poverty of the populace, Headley wanted to hang the king "on one of his own oaks."[3]

But the notion that art was executed at the "expense of food for the poor" softened as America approached the mid-nineteenth century. The fine arts became a legitimate source of pleasure. Ralph Waldo Emerson expressed a growing sensuous delight in beauty, declaring: "Rome is a grand town and works mightily upon the senses and upon the soul."[4]

A growing use of ornament was certainly noticeable in New Orleans during the 1850s. In 1856 the *New Orleans Daily Crescent* noted the rising tide of the Italianate taste: "We may remark that the plain fashion of building has almost entirely gone out of vogue. Not only the public buildings display the finest designs of the architect, but the residences and stores are also elegantly ornamented; the residences being put up in different styles of fanciful architecture. . . ."[5]

In America as a whole the domestic Italianate took several forms. There were symmetrical, square-fronted houses of two or three stories designed to resemble palazzi. Another type, designed to resemble Italian villas, consisted of asymmetrical, rambling houses with copious verandas and often a tower. Then there were the folk versions of the style. A three-story boxy farmhouse enlivened with Italianate details on the porch and around the roof was once a common sight in the rural parts of the East and Midwest.

In assessing the Italianate heritage of Louisiana, one must begin with two general statements: 1) that the style here deviated significantly from the national norm, at least on the domestic side, and 2) that, with the exception of fairly late commercial buildings, the style did not have a great deal of impact outside New Orleans.

The *New Orleans Daily Picayune* of September 19, 1850, described a new house for Duncan Hennen as an "Italian villa." This is the first known specific reference in the city to the Italianate taste.[6] In the succeeding years a limited number of stately symmetrical palazzi were built in New Orleans. But as Caldwell points out, the palazzo mode, being essentially a "flirtation with the East Coast and British influences," was not native to the area and was never very popular.[7] Also unpopular was the Italian villa. Although some villa-like houses were built, they were tame in comparison with those found elsewhere in the country, almost invariably lacking a tower and being only minimally asymmetrical. In short, they lacked the dramatic silhouette normally associated with Italian villas.

Although Louisianians were not overly receptive to Italian palazzi and villas, they certainly embraced the Italianate style as a whole. In contrast to the national norm, the Italianate in Louisiana, at least for residences, was very much a columnar form, with Italian details and features grafted onto local symmetrical house types such as the two-story galleried house and the traditional raised galleried cottage. These familiar forms had never been so richly and elaborately clothed as they were during the heyday of the Italianate taste.

In understanding Italianate domestic architecture in Louisiana, it is useful to contrast it with its predecessor, the Greek Revival. In a way, both styles ultimately trace their origins to classical antiquity, and both rely upon the column and the entablature as primary architectural features. But while the Greek Revival tended to be plain, almost severe, the Italianate was richly ornamented, featuring a complex interplay of numerous individual members. The analogy of a wedding cake comes to mind. Also, the Italianate had features of its own that were not found in the Greek Revival, including round-arch windows and doors, segmentally arched

Designed by Charles Hillger in 1869, the asymmetrical John Blaffer House in New Orleans features the hesitant suggestion of a tower of the kind often found on Italianate villas. Photo by Donna Fricker.

Above left: This 1840s two-story Greek Revival galleried house in New Orleans makes an interesting contrast with the Italianate example to the right. Above right: This New Orleans Italianate galleried house (c. 1860) is richly styled with arched openings, prominent brackets and quoins (decorative blocks at the corners designed to resemble cut stone). Contrasting it with the Greek Revival example to the left reveals a considerable change in taste within a roughly twenty-year period. Photos by Donna Fricker.

openings, and Italian double-arched windows. Other distinctive features include copious panels and quoins, parapets with curving tops, and galleries that curve in the Roman fashion.

There is little doubt that the hallmark of the Italianate style is the decorative bracket. Developed from Roman decorative supports called consoles, brackets are found on a wide variety of Italianate buildings. Often they are set in pairs over columns or between the upper windows on commercial buildings. As the Italianate progressed through the decades, brackets tended to grow in size, occasionally reaching half a story in height.

Italianate domestic interiors were sumptuous, featuring rich and heavy decorative moldings around the ceiling. These were combined with cast plaster ornament in a variety of naturalistic designs such as vine and grape. Hissing gas chandeliers hung from ornate ceiling medallions. The focus of any room was the fireplace with its round-arch Italian mantel which was often of marble or slate or cast-iron painted to resemble marble. John Maass in his book on Victorian taste, *The*

Gingerbread Age, exaggerated somewhat in describing such an interior. He noted that the windows were "barricaded with a fivefold layer of shutters, blinds, muslin curtains, velvet draperies and tasseled valances." "A floral carpet is underfoot," wrote Maass, "and large-figured wallpaper all around; there are overstuffed chairs, tufted ottomans, marble-topped tables and carved sideboards; the remaining space is garnished with potted plants, bronzed statuary, plaster casts, wax flowers under glass domes, shellwork, beadwork, fringed cushions, gilt-framed pictures and petit-point mottoes; souvenirs and bric-a-brac are ranged on fretwork brackets and tiered whatnots."[8]

To a fair extent ornate interiors of this kind were brought about thanks to inexpensive household goods made possible by Victorian manufacturing technology.

Detail of classical scroll consoles, Palazzo Farnese, Rome, begun 1514. Photo by Donna Fricker.

This same technology marked the exterior of Italianate buildings as well, for it was through the Italianate style that manufactured cast iron came into its own as a building medium. By the mid-nineteenth century, there were several large iron foundries in the New Orleans area. Firms such as Leeds and Company, Reynolds Iron Works, and Shakespeare Iron Works turned out everything from steam engines to gun carriages. They also manufactured various lines of decorative porch columns, balconies and balustrades.[9] These architectural elements could be ordered with a wide variety of motifs, including baroque scrolls, bunches of flowers and fruits, interlocking arches, and vine and grape designs, to name just a few. It was during the Italianate age that one saw galleries formed of large panels of lacy ironwork. An interesting fact is that the much noted cast-iron galleries in the French Quarter date largely from this period. Although they are often regarded as part of the French character of the place, most of them, in fact, reflect the Italianate taste, which was an import from Britain. It is also important to note that while cast-iron galleries or porches were found throughout the country, they were more prevalent in New Orleans and were a much more prominent feature, often taking over the entire facade of a building.

Galleries also graced many of Louisiana's Italianate commercial buildings,

Above: 1433 Philip St., New Orleans. Built in 1856 and possibly remodeled c. 1880, this is the traditional Louisiana raised galleried cottage in flamboyant Italianate dress, featuring over-sized column capitals, double brackets, an extremely lively parapet and large arched dormers. Below: Bracketed shotgun houses (c. 1890), Camp St., New Orleans. Photos by Donna Fricker.

Nottoway Plantation House, Iberville Parish, was designed by Henry Howard and his partner Albert Diettel in 1858. With its enormous size, rambling asymmetrical design, curving gallery and boldly formed pillars and brackets, it is the closest thing Louisiana has to an Italianate villa. Photo by Donna Fricker.

although most have since been removed. On the whole these buildings were similar to those built in other parts of the country with cast-iron and plate-glass shopfronts on the first story and rows of ornamented windows on the upper stories. All of this was capped by a richly decorated, oversized cornice. Often the window moldings were of cast iron as well. Grand and humble versions of the standard Italianate commercial building can be found in many communities throughout the state. The largest and finest surviving collections are in New Orleans and Shreveport.

As the decade of the 1880s dawned, the Italianate was passing out of fashion in America. However, the style would enjoy a vigorous posthumous existence for another twenty years or so

An Italianate doorway in the Lower Garden District of New Orleans. Photo by Donna Fricker.

Nottoway Plantation House is an excellent place to view elaborate Italianate interior details. Photo by Donna Fricker.

in Louisiana. Commercial buildings in the Italianate style continued to be built until after the turn of the century. In addition, the New Orleans shotgun house tradition created a whole new generation of exuberant Italianate houses, mostly speculatively built. Although cottages share similar details, the Italianate shotgun has become almost a signature of New Orleans. With elaborate sinuous brackets, segmentally arched windows and decoratively cut boards on the front, these houses, surviving by the thousands, add much to the character of the city. Architectural features were manufactured by firms such as Robert Roberts Steam Sash and Door Company. Of course, these features were no longer conceived of as Italian; rather they had become part of the standard builder's vocabulary.

Amorphous as it may be, the Italianate style represents a very significant chapter in the history of taste both in the country as a whole and in Louisiana. Until about twenty-five years ago, it, like all other manifestations of the Victorian Age, was in deep disgrace. One gentleman described his old Italianate house as "large but not roomy . . . fancy but not beautiful . . . orderly in a littered sort of way," and "consistent in that nothing belonged where it was."[10] But more recently attitudes have changed. Worn out with the rectilinear sterility of modern construction, people have increasingly turned to the Italianate for its richness and fanciful feeling, characteristics for which it was admired in the first place.

Cast-iron gallery detail, New Orleans, 1896. During the Italianate period, ornate cast-iron became a popular substitute for wooden columns. Photo by Donna Fricker.

Although the Italianate style Bruslé Building (1889) in Plaquemine rivals in quality some found in larger cities, most Italianate structures in small town Louisiana were much less elaborate. Photo by Donna Fricker.

The Eastlake Style

by Jonathan Fricker

Few men have had the distinction of giving their names to styles of architecture and fewer still have done so under protest. Such was the case with British architect Charles Lock Eastlake. He was part of a generation of Victorian moralists who believed in the spiritual value of art and furnishings. Deploring the low state to which taste had fallen in mid-nineteenth century England, he set about to reform it. Eastlake hated anything he considered flashy, sham or showy, preferring objects plainly made in a straightforward manner with natural materials, to use his word, "sincere." He recommended furniture designed in the medieval way with pegs to hold the various members together. After all, a peg was "sincere," a nail was not.[1] His furniture featured straight wood members, table legs and spindles turned on a lathe and delicate ornamental motifs.[2]

In 1868 Eastlake published a thin book called *Hints on Household Taste* which became vastly popular in Britain and in particular in America. Indeed, it went through many printings. Here were attractive designs with a powerful moral philosophy behind them. Eastlake became a household word and a messiah of good taste on both sides of the Atlantic. *Harper's Bazaar* reported: "Suddenly the voice of the prophet Eastlake was heard crying in the wilderness. Repent ye, for the Kingdom of the Tasteful is at hand!"[3]

The idea that "sincere" artistic interiors could give a spiritual boost had a wide appeal in Victorian America. As Russell Lynes wrote in *The Tastemakers:* "Here was a chance not only to redecorate but to be saved at the same time."[4] Moreover, tastefulness was good for human relations. American socialite and Eastlake disciple Mrs. M. E. W. Sherwood put it bluntly: "Who knows how much incompatibility of temper, sorrow, passionate discontent, mutual disgust may not have grown out of . . . unhappy surroundings? Nay . . . divorce laws may be perhaps directly traced to some frightful inharmoniousness in wallpaper. The soothing influence of an Eastlake bookcase on an irritated husband has never been sufficiently calculated. . . ." "We must have beauty around us to make us good," she concluded.[5]

But despite Eastlake's meteoric rise to popularity, there were problems. American manufacturers were not exactly following his tasteful lead. In 1878 he wrote: "I find American tradesmen continually advertising what they are pleased to call

Eastlake furniture, a plate from *Hints on Household Taste,* which first appeared in England in 1868 and in America in 1872. Reproduced with permission of Dover Publications, Inc.

'Eastlake' furniture, with the production of which I have nothing whatever to do, and for the taste of which I should be very sorry to be considered responsible."[6]

But American carpenters and builders went beyond mere furniture. In their exuberance they enlarged upon Eastlake's lathe turned structural members and decorative cuts to create a new style of architecture. Elaborately turned gallery columns resembled table legs. Rows of turned spindles formed screens atop porches. Curved brackets appeared in profusion as did dowel rods, knobs, and circular forms resembling portions of wagon wheels. These features were fundamentally three dimensional, a characteristic that distinguished them from the two dimensional jigsaw brackets of the late Italianate style.

Eastlake gallery at Glencoe, 1897, East Feliciana Parish. Note the turned columns (in many ways the signature of the style) and the abacus-like spindlework. Photo by Donna Fricker.

Eastlake was a style of decoration in contrast to a complete style of architecture involving massing and other components. It was a collection of features (turned columns, brackets, spindlework, etc.) that could be applied to buildings of various types. And applied it was during the 1880s and '90s, with effects that were every bit as exuberant and fanciful as the Italianate.

Mr. Eastlake was not pleased. In 1882 he fired off a hot letter to America: "I now find, to my amazement, that there exists on the other side of the Atlantic an 'Eastlake style' of architecture, which, judging from the specimens I have seen illustrated, may be said to burlesque such doctrines of art as I have ventured to

Above: Eastlake column, brackets, and spindlework, New Orleans. Photo by Donna Fricker.

maintain. . . . I feel greatly flattered by the popularity which my books have attained in America, but I regret that their author's name should be associated there with a phase of taste in architecture and industrial art with which I can have no real sympathy, and which by all accounts seems to be extravagant and bizarre."[7]

Bizarre or not, the Eastlake style enjoyed a vast popularity in Louisiana, with examples surviving by the thousands and sometimes representing an area's earliest architectural heritage. The style's emphasis upon ornamenting the veranda suited our galleried house tradition ideally. In addition, turned spindles and columns and curved brackets were easy to manufacture and could be produced by the trainload in the various industrial lumber mills which were springing up in Louisiana in the 1880s and '90s.

In the New Orleans area a whole new genera-

Typical New Orleans Eastlake double shotgun, c. 1890.
Photo by Robert J. Cangelosi.

Above: Intricate Eastlake decorative panel spanning the hallway of the Ransonet House (1898), Breaux Bridge, St. Martin Parish. Below: A close look at the gable of the Eastlake entrance porch, Ransonet House. Photos by Donna Fricker.

tion of shotgun houses appeared sporting Eastlake porches with turned columns and curving brackets. The Louisiana Creole cottage tradition continued into the Eastlake era. But instead of chamfered columns of the kind found on c. 1820 examples, these new up-to-date galleries were fitted with turned Eastlake columns and sometimes bands of spindles. The style also made its way into Louisiana interiors. Often this took the form of decorative screens of knobs, rods and other members sometimes known as "carpenter's lace."

By the early years of this century the Eastlake craze had more or less run its course in Louisiana. By mid-century it was regarded by modernists as a particularly unsightly reminder of the much despised Victorian age. Ironically, Eastlake's philosophy of sincerity and the use of natural materials was rather like their own. It was the same philosophy applied with completely different results.

Charles Eastlake made several contributions to the world of art, but nothing that rivaled the prominence of the style of architecture he inadvertently created. Ultimately he became keeper and secretary of Britain's National Gallery and worked to classify pictures according to the schools to which they belonged, an innovation at the time. He also wrote a respected history of the Gothic Revival in architecture. Eastlake lived until 1906, enough time to see his bastard style pass from the forefront of fashion.[8] It is indeed ironic that the supreme contribution of his life was the one of which he himself was the least proud.

Eastlake ornamented gable peak in Breaux Bridge. Photo by Donna Fricker.

The Queen Anne Revival Style

by Donna Fricker

If ever there was a misnamed style, it was the Queen Anne Revival. One would logically think it to be a revival of the architecture popular in England during the reign of Queen Anne (1702-1714). However, Queen Anne would not see much similarity between the architecture of her reign and the style that emerged under her name in England in the 1870s. The style as it developed in America would be completely beyond recognition.

The Queen Anne Revival, like William Morris wallpapers and Eastlake furniture, was the product of the so-called "aesthetic movement," an art craze that swept England and America during the 1870s and 1880s. Some have called the move-

Watts Sherman House, Newport, Rhode Island, 1874, H. H. Richardson, Architect. Photo by Donna Fricker.

42

ment an escape from a world of shoddy flashy manufactured goods and bleak depressing buildings. Others point to it as a reaction by artists and architects against the fierce moral strictures of the Gothic Revival. One writer has called it simply the "religion of beauty."[1]

Eclectic in its taste, the aesthetic movement valued art for its own sake, glorying in finely crafted furniture, exquisite Persian rugs, fine Japanese prints and picturesque English cottages. It bespoke a quiet contemplative life where one was surrounded by beautiful and curious objects in an "aesthetical" setting. Like the Gothic Revival, the aesthetic movement held that there was a spiritual charge to be had from beautiful things.

The spirit of the movement was best summarized in a satirical cartoon appearing in *Punch*. In it a pair of newlyweds are examining a wedding present, an artistic teapot. The groom remarks: "It is quite consummate, is it not!" To this the intense bride replies: "It is indeed! Oh, Algernon, let us live up to it!"[2]

Art even had the power to inspire and cultivate untasteful persons. In 1882, the *Burlington* wrote a satirical piece about a Mr. Philistine Jones who moves into a Queen Anne Revival house after which his taste improves.[3]

Mr. Jones' Queen Anne house was created by borrowing parts from various historic periods. Architectural historian Mark Girouard has aptly referred to the English Queen Anne as an "architectural cocktail," while another author, Russell Lynes, termed it a "tossed salad."[4] While there might be a little genuine Queen Anne in a given example, there might also be motifs from two or three centuries of English architecture as well as some Dutch and Flemish influence. The overriding concern, writes Walter C. Kidney, was "to create something comfortable and charming, using anything and everything that served the purpose."[5] Various names were suggested at the time for this "architectural cocktail," but Queen Anne was the one that stuck, according to Girouard, "for no very good reason."[6]

The Queen Anne appeared in various forms in England. The style's leading architect, Richard Norman Shaw, provided the model that was initially copied in America by architects and then interpreted by builders. Shaw designed asymmetrical late-medieval-looking manor houses featuring steeply pitched prominent gables, half-timbering and tile sheathing in the upper stories. Half-timbering, a popular method of construction in sixteenth- and seventeenth-century England, consisted of heavy, irregularly placed exposed timbers with plaster infill. In the Queen Anne Revival, the wooden members were decorative rather than structural.

Shaw's work was well known and much admired in America. Popular acceptance of the style was aided immeasurably by the 1876 Centennial Exposition in Philadelphia, with two half-timbered buildings erected by the British government receiving rave reviews in the architectural press.

The style made its debut in America in 1874 with the Watts Sherman House in Newport, Rhode Island. Designed by H. H. Richardson, the house closely resembled

Lewis House, 1899, Shreveport, one of Louisiana's finest
Queen Anne Revival houses. Photo by Donna Fricker.

the work of Shaw, but with wooden shingles instead of tiles. Various high style East Coast architect-designed examples followed, largely in the Shaw tradition, and by the 1880s the style was becoming popular around the country. As it devel-

Rose Lawn, Natchitoches, 1903, George Barber and Thomas Kluttz, Architects.
Photo by Donna Fricker.

oped and was interpreted by builders, it took on a distinctly different look, although the design principles were the same.

Whether in England or America, whether architect designed or vernacular, the Queen Anne Revival is a style which achieves a picturesque look through irregularity, both in massing and surface textures. In America, the building materials were often different, the massing was typically more complex, and new ingredients were added to the "architectural cocktail" or "tossed salad."

High spirited and free-wheeling, the Queen Anne Revival in America followed the Victorian dictum that "too much is never enough." Wild silhouettes were created by projections of various sorts going in various directions—multiple gables, polygonal bays, balconies, dormers, prominent chimneys, etc.—anything to avoid a boring roofline and plain flat walls. The ultimate projection was a turret—a round, polygonal or square tower typically set at the corner and rising above the roofline. Unknown in the English Queen Anne, this feature is believed by some to have been borrowed from French châteaux.

Further irregularity was created by using various materials of different textures. In the East, for example, a house might have a stone or brick first floor, a

Above: Paul Billeaud House, Broussard, 1911.
Below: Andrus House, Jennings, ca. 1895. Photos by Donna Fricker.

Above: Reeder-Garland House, Bernice, ca. 1903.
Below: Patin House, Breaux Bridge, ca. 1895, a good example of the Queen Anne
as it typically appears in Louisiana. Photos by Donna Fricker.

clapboarded second story, and wooden shingles (the American equivalent of English tiles) in various patterns covering projecting bays. In Louisiana, and much of the United States, Queen Anne houses are invariably of wood; hence the textures are not as varied. A typical Louisiana example is clapboarded with shingles in the gable peaks. The more patterns used, the richer the textured effect. A small minority feature half-timbering or sunburst motifs in the gables.

Additional visual interest is provided by porches which often wrap around the side of the house. If there is a turret or other protrusion the gallery curves to follow the shape. Porches are more often than not in the Eastlake style, featuring turned columns and bands of spindlework. Polygonal bays and gable peaks might also be decorated with Eastlake motifs. Popularly known today as "gingerbread," Eastlake ornamentation was a distinctly American phenomenon and added greatly to the very different look the Queen Anne acquired in this country.

The Queen Anne produced a strikingly vertical house, typically of two or two-and-a-half stories. Verticality was further emphasized by elements such as steeply pitched gables and roofs, turrets and prominent tall chimneys. However, in Louisiana and other parts of the Deep South there was a marked fondness for one and one-and-a-half story rambling Queen Anne galleried cottages. Even with a turret, such a house is fundamentally horizontal. In Louisiana, at least, Queen Anne elements such as polygonal bays were often grafted onto the standard galleried cottage.

Also, on the whole, Louisiana Queen Anne houses are fairly conservative in massing and ornamentation when compared to the national norm. While the state has scores of perfectly splendid eye-popping Queen Anne houses, the more typical example is a modest one-story cottage with a polygonal forward-facing bay, an Eastlake gallery that perhaps wraps around the side, and shingling in the gables.

The Queen Anne enjoyed great popularity in America into the first decade of this century. Here was a "user friendly" style that was imminently adaptable without exacting requirements. It could be built by any carpenter using an architect's plans, pattern books, or perhaps just his and the client's imagination. After all, was there really a wrong way to build such an eclectic house?[7]

Queen Anne houses survive in Louisiana by the thousands, making an immense contribution to the character of our historic built environment. Fortunately, they are quite popular among today 's old house buffs, being bought and restored by the droves. And why not? Where else could you find not only a delightful style, but one named for a queen who would not recognize it?

The Colonial Revival Style

by Jonathan Fricker

Henry James in 1879 wrote: "History, as yet, has left in the United States but so thin and impalpable a deposit that we very soon touch the hard substratum of nature."[1] America was a young country bursting onto the expanding western frontier. But even as James wrote these words things were changing. For it was with the aftermath of the Civil War, and the coming of the centennial celebration in 1876, that it occurred to Americans that they had a past, one just distant and rosy enough to be attractive.

Historians have pointed to several factors in the wave of nostalgia that swept the nation: 1) the increasingly fast pace of life in our industrialized cities, 2) the notorious scandals surrounding the administration of President Grant, and 3) the increasing practice of Easterners to vacation in the early colonial towns of New England.

In 1881 the noted Philadelphia architect George C. Mason observed: "No wonder we are ready to step back a hundred years into the past, to the good old days when George the Third was King, [and] when stately men and women glided through life in quiet dignity." Mason urged his fellow architects to study "humbly and earnestly" the buildings of our colonial past.[2]

What is probably America's first neo-colonial house was built in 1876 in Elberton, New Jersey, and it set the tone for eastern Colonial Revival houses that were to follow. It did not much resemble real colonial houses which were considered by Victorian standards to be small, inconvenient and uncomfortable. Rather it was a conventional Victorian house fitted up with colonial details such as classical columns and elliptical arches. In other examples additional colonial features would be used such as classical modillion cornices and Palladian windows. As time went on, the Colonial Revival became more sober and boxy, dispensing with its Victorian asymmetrical massing. These large somewhat uninteresting houses were nonetheless comfortable and convenient, as Walter Kidney has described them, houses designed "to be lived in rather than looked at."[3]

The Nicholas Burke House in New Orleans (1896, Toledano and Wogan) is awash with Colonial Revival details, including three-dimensional swags of flowers hanging from the column capitals. Photo by Donna Fricker.

Swan-neck pedimented dor-
mer on the Burke House.
Note also the modillion cornice highlighting the eaves.
Beneath the modillion cornice
is a denticular band. Photo by
Donna Fricker.

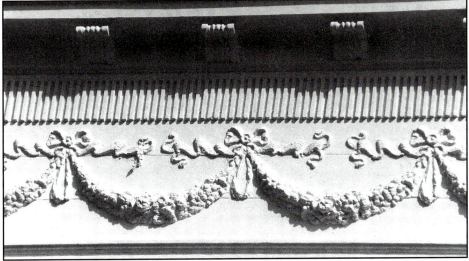

Swags of flowers accenting the Burke House. Photo by Donna Fricker.

Because the colonial style was perceived by and large as a native American style, its revival gained impetus from the rising tide of American nationalism. It dovetailed well with turn-of-the-century America, an age characterized by do-or-die patriotism, lavish Fourth of July pyrotechnical displays, John Philip Sousa marches, and an overall atmosphere of blustering jingoism.

In this vein, various writers imbued the colonial style with a kind of nativist idealism which rested upon the notion that the architecture of the thirteen colonies was somehow fundamentally different from traditional English architecture. In truth, most American colonial architecture is closely related to the English Georgian style, a classical style that took its name from the reigns of Kings George I, II, and III. But in this patriotic view, colonial buildings were seen as much the product of native American ingenuity as of European tradition. For example, in an article on the Southern colonies published in 1916, Frank E. Wallis asserted that our colonial was "the son of the Georgian, if you please." American carpenters and joiners had plied the Georgian style with an originality and an exuberance "as would have shocked the stolid Britishers of the Georgian times."[4]

But, if the Colonial Revival was a symbol of our national pride, it was a rather poorly defined one, both in the minds of architects and the general public. Anything the least bit old and venerable could be dubbed "colonial," ranging from the

Cook House (1904), Alexandria. Photo by Jim Zietz.

medieval-looking homes of the Pilgrim fathers, to Cape Cod cottages, to Georgian mansions in Virginia, even to 1840s Greek Revival plantation houses in Louisiana. All were covered by the nebulous term "colonial."

With one notable exception (the shotgun house), Louisiana's experience with the Colonial Revival paralleled that of other states in the Deep South. In the early phase (c. 1895-1905), conventional Queen Anne Revival houses with asymmetrical massing were fitted with colonial style features. The Nicholas Burke House at 5809 St. Charles Avenue in New Orleans is probably Louisiana's most spectacular example. Designed in 1896 by Toledano and Wogan, the house features a boldly curving gallery with coupled classical columns surmounted by an entablature with heavily sculpted swags of leaves and flowers. The sharply jutting second story porch has a large Palladian doorway of the type that appeared on many Georgian houses. There are several long runs of balustrade punctuated by newel posts with urns on top. The house culminates in an energetic roofline with prominent dormers capped by flamboyantly over-sized swan-neck pediments. The curving swan-neck pediment, a feature associated with the period of Sir Christopher Wren, was popular for doorways on grander colonial houses. Although striking in its use of colonial features, the Burke House still retains the picturesque asymmetrical shape associated with Queen Anne Revival architecture. Clearly it is a Queen Anne game played with colonial markers.

Another good example of this transitional phase is the Cook House in Alexandria. Although eight years later than the Burke House, it is even more Queen Anne in massing, complete with a prominent side tower. Its detailing, however, is Colonial Revival, including classical columns (instead of Eastlake), swags accenting the tower, and a Palladian window in the front dormer.

During the first decade of this century the classical aspect of the Colonial Revival began to dominate in Louisiana. Massing became quieter. Houses became boxy and symmetrical and made frequent use of prominent white columns of both one and two stories. A favorite device was to have a one-story porch running across the front of the house with a superimposed two-story monumental portico.

Some Colonial Revival residences began to bear a striking resemblance to antebellum Greek Revival houses. Viewed from the front, the Governor Luther Hall House in Monroe definitely presents this appearance. But upon closer inspection, certain aspects of the house give it away. The portico is rather large for the facade, the pediment is a bit more vertical than an antebellum one would have been, and the columns are not evenly spaced. Moreover, features such as plate-glass windows could not possibly be antebellum. In truth, the house was built in 1906. It is interesting to note that it was referred to as a "delightful old Colonial home" in a 1929 article in the *Monroe Morning World*. [5] "Old Colonial," indeed! At the time the house was scarcely twenty-three years old.

Large white-columned houses such as the Hall House reminded Southerners

Angelus (1907), Jennings. Photo by Donna Fricker.

of the region's antebellum past, which was becoming increasingly romanticized in the late nineteenth and early twentieth centuries. This nostalgia for the glory days before the Civil War was noted by visiting British playwright Oscar Wilde: "Among the more elderly inhabitants of the South I found a melancholy tendency to date every event of importance on the late War, 'How beautiful the moon is tonight,' I once remarked to a gentleman standing near me. 'Yes,' was his reply, 'but you should have seen it before the War. ' "[6]

In addition to relatively grand houses such as the Luther Hall House, the Colonial Revival produced another generation of shotgun houses. These new "colonial" shotguns, located in New Orleans and vicinity, had squarish fronts; sometimes richly ornamented entablatures; and importantly, round classical columns. As with other periods in the New Orleans shotgun-house tradition, these Colonial Revival shotguns represent a unique collection. While shotguns are found throughout the South, they are typically humble, unadorned buildings. By contrast, New Orleans shotguns are usually richly styled.

After the First World War, America embarked upon a new scholarly phase of the Colonial Revival, one more correct from the antiquarian standpoint. It produced houses which truly resembled real colonial buildings, at least from the exterior. It was during these years that the Rockefeller Foundation undertook the painstaking (by the standard of the time) restoration of Colonial Williamsburg. Historic

2222 Government St., c. 1910, Baton Rouge. Note the Palladian windows flanking the entrance porch. Photo by Donna Fricker.

Luther Hall House (1906), Monroe, William Drago, Architect. Photo by Donna Fricker.

preservation laws began to be passed protecting historic districts, one of the earliest being the 1936 creation of the Vieux Carré Commission in New Orleans.

This new approach received a good deal of impetus from *The White Pines Series of Architectural Monographs,* a monthly magazine published by the White Pines Institute between 1916 and 1929. Although its ostensible purpose was to encourage the use of white pine in construction, it also published scholarly and semi-scholarly articles on Colonial American architecture as well as plans and measured drawings of colonial buildings. Also published were designs for modern buildings in which features

An early house in the Minden Historic District which was remodeled in the Mount Vernon Colonial Revival style, c. 1930. Photo by Donna Fricker.

were taken from specific colonial prototypes. This architectural series is widely held to have been a leading influence in shaping the character of American Colonial Revival architecture of the 1920s and 1930s.

A favorite feature to copy was George Washington's huge and ungainly portico at Mount Vernon. Improved in proportion by the skilled hands of trained architects, the Mount Vernon portico became the hallmark of literally thousands of Colonial Revival houses coast to coast. Several dozen survive in Louisiana as do other manifestations of the "correct colonial style." But on the whole, this more refined and scholarly mode of the Colonial Revival had less impact here than it did in the eastern states. It was certainly never as popular as the contemporaneous Bungalow style.

Colonial Revival houses, built during an era of nostalgia, are now themselves the objects of nostalgia. They look older than they are, in some cases conjuring up images of our antebellum past. Some examples are nearing a hundred years of age. These buildings are important to us both for their considerable architectural qualities and the interesting period they represent.

Colonial Revival shotgun house in the Mid-City Historic District,
New Orleans, built c. 1910.
Photo by Donna Fricker.

The Beaux Arts
and Neo-Classical Styles

by Patricia L. Duncan

The concept of a renaissance or rebirth is most closely associated with the end of the so-called "Dark Ages" beginning in the fifteenth century, when Europe turned away from its medieval heritage and sought the glorious civilization of ancient Rome. However, some historians believe that a renaissance occurred in American architecture around the end of the nineteenth century.[1] This American renaissance centered upon the renewed use of classical elements from Greece and Rome in the design of buildings which were meant to serve as monuments for all time. Two styles—the Beaux Arts and the Neo-Classical—comprised this renaissance.

Classical motifs include lintels, pediments, colonnades, the orders of column capitals, arches, and vaults. Over the centuries these elements have remained a mainstay of architectural design. Although not the first generation to turn to classical antiquity for inspiration, Italian Renaissance builders used its motifs to create palaces and churches which inspired subsequent generations of builders throughout the Western World. Thus, the influence of classical and Renaissance architecture can be traced through the Baroque, Georgian, Federal, Early Classical Revival, and Greek Revival styles. Although classicism temporarily lost favor during the more flamboyant Victorian age, it found renewed popularity at the end of the nineteenth century. Three related factors contributed to this re-emergence in the United States. These developments were the desire to commemorate the achievements of the Gilded Age, a revolt against the design excesses of the Victorian era, and the 1893 world's fair.[2]

Historians tend to view the Gilded Age as a negative period marked by greed, political scandals, and the rise of monster trusts. Nevertheless, Americans who experienced the post-Civil War period firsthand saw it as an optimistic era of prosperity and progress. As had past generations, they chose to commemorate their nation's wealth, self-confidence, and maturity through architecture. As a result the Gilded Age saw the construction of a large number of impressive, monumental

The Beaux Arts Scottish Rite Cathedral, Shreveport, 1915, Edward F. Neild, Architect. Photo courtesy of Noel Memorial Library, Archives and Special Collections, LSU-Shreveport, Chamber of Commerce Collection, Bill Grabill, photographer.

public buildings such as courthouses, libraries, schools, and railway stations. But as this remarkable epoch reached its golden afternoon, the colorful, wildly textured, aggressively picturesque High Victorian piles that had been its hallmark fell out of fashion. Instead, the establishment turned increasingly to the grandeur of classical antiquity to show off its wealth and power.

This turn toward classicism was led by a recently emerged cadre of highly educated professional architects. Until the mid-nineteenth century, America had few academically

Right: The Beaux Arts Ruston State Bank, 1910. Photo by Donna Fricker.

trained builders. Instead, buildings were constructed by carpenter-businessmen who copied design motifs from builders' handbooks or obtained on-the-job experience under master builders. This situation began to change only after Richard Morris Hunt became the first of a group of Americans to study at France's École des Beaux Arts at mid-century. Established under Napoleon Bonaparte to monitor and encourage French arts and architecture, the École emphasized a design philosophy based upon monumentality, symmetry, unity, formality, restraint, and importance of "composition." Furthermore, École students were taught to look to the classical past for design inspiration. It was these French-trained American École graduates, and the students whom they in turn taught, who would decree American architectural tastes at the nineteenth century's end.

The influence of the École and the rebellion against Victorian design were reinforced by the World's Columbian Exposition of 1893. Nicknamed the "White City" because of its shimmering all white color scheme, this world's fair featured monumental central buildings which were grouped around a lagoon, conformed to a uniform cornice height, and displayed classical decoration. Said one enthusiast, the Chicago fair ". . . was simply the best single monument to the United States and its art to that time or since."[3] However, proponents of modern architecture have universally denigrated the fair because, according to their world view, it " . . . condemned American architecture to the imitative and derivative for another generation."[4] Nevertheless, the widely publicized and attended fair influenced building design for almost a half century.

The early phase of this return to classical antiquity is known as the Beaux Arts style. It was an eclectic architectural tradition characterized by monumentality, majestic axial plans, projecting pavilions, free-standing statuary, colossal columns (often paired) and other exuberant surface decoration based on classical and Renaissance motifs. Although Greek orders were sometimes used, Roman prototypes, with their imperial associations, were preferred.

The Beaux Arts differed from previous classical revivals in that its buildings were larger and its surface ornament more vibrant and elaborate. However, after about 1900 a preference for quieter, less theatrical, and more refined forms emerged. This new style became known as the Neo-Classical. Its defining features included rectangular masses with large expanses of plain wall surfaces lacking projections, an absence of free-standing statues, single rather than coupled columns, white or at least light coloration, and a preference for Greek rather than Roman precedents. The latter is seen in the style's tendency to use linteled openings rather than arched openings.

While competing with the Beaux Arts for popularity in local courthouse and city hall design, the Neo-Classical became the style of choice for federal and state government buildings. Architects developed standard approaches to their design. One popular formula was the building whose massive, rusticated basement

The classical design of the Calcasieu Parish Courthouse (1912, Favrot and Livaudais) is derived mainly from Roman sources. Photo by Donna Fricker.

anchored a multi-story office block standing behind colossal columns or pilasters supporting an entablature. This design was eventually used for many building types. Another approach, popular for state capitols, was the domed structure with wings reflecting legislative branches. Although architects eventually stripped its ornament to a bare minimum, the Neo-Classical style continued to be used on federal buildings long after more modern styles gained the ascendancy in American architecture. One critic has called these later structures "pompous nests of officials" lacking "an air of welcome and life."[5]

Neo-Classical buildings can usually be distinguished from those of the earlier Greek Revival style by their size. However, it is easy to confuse the Neo-Classical with the Colonial Revival because, in addition to their use of similar classical elements, they were popular at the same time. Nevertheless, the philosophical underpinnings, and at least some of the design precedents, were different. The Colonial Revival was an American style which evolved as a response to the growing patriotism of the Gilded Age. Its design inspiration stemmed from colonial and early American buildings, only some of which used classical forms. The Colonial Revival also included elements which are non-classical—salt box and gambrel roofed houses come immediately to mind. The Neo-Classical style was an international movement which was the logical culmination of the repeated "discovery" of classical

The Neo-Classical Ouachita National Bank, Monroe, 1906, Drago and Smith, Architects. Photo by Donna Fricker.

The Neo-Classical Bolton High School, Alexandria, 1926, Favrot and Livaudais, Architects.
Photo by Donna Fricker.

design elements over the centuries. Grander than the Colonial Revival, it was used primarily for monumental public and institutional buildings.

Louisiana's Beaux Arts and Neo-Classical buildings resemble those in the rest of the nation. The styles were used mostly for courthouses, banks and schools. For example, the courthouses in Allen, Beauregard, and DeSoto parishes reflect the Beaux Arts taste. With its paired colossal columns, arched as well as linteled openings, statuary, and abundance of flamboyant classical ornament, Shreveport's monumental Scottish Rite Cathedral (1915) is one of the state's most outstanding Beaux Arts buildings. Lincoln Parish's Ruston State Bank (1910) is also an important example. In addition to the paired pilasters, its Beaux Arts features include an entrance combining the idea of a Roman triumphal arch with that of a classical temple front, a flamboyant and over-scaled coffered barrel vault which breaks through the entablature above it, and excessive sculpted decoration in the spandrels of the arch and the tympanum of the pediment.

There are a dozen or so parish courthouses in the Neo-Classical style. Baton Rouge has a fine Neo-Classical railway station (1925). Despite the presence of arched openings on the facade, the preponderance of Greek elements on Monroe's Ouachita National Bank (1906) place it squarely within the Neo-Classical style. With its rusticated basement story and colossal columns, Alexandria's Bolton High School (1926) is a prime example of the popular multi-story design formula frequently found on government buildings. Its severe ornament indicates that it was constructed during the later phase of Neo-Classical design. Shreveport's old Municipal Court Building (1924) is an even more restrained example. In addition to its use in buildings, the Neo-Classical proved to be a popular style for New Orleans' above-ground tombs.

Unfortunately, some of Louisiana's Beaux Arts and Neo-Classical buildings stand vacant and threatened by demolition because their designs are deemed impractical for today's business and educational needs. However, many survive as the cherished monuments to progress which their builders intended them to be.

The Neo-Classical Municipal Court Building, Shreveport, 1924, Edward F. Neild, Architect.
Photo by Donna Fricker.

The Bungalow Style

by Patricia L Duncan

The arrival of the twentieth century brought a major change to the American housing market. Home builders and purchasers alike abandoned their preference for the formal and overly ornate Victorian home in favor of a smaller and simpler house designed to meet the needs of middle-class families. This economical new home, called the bungalow, would make home ownership a reality for thousands of Americans.

As we know it today, the bungalow is a simple, low, horizontal, and informal dwelling. Its defining features include prominent roof gables, overhanging eaves with exposed rafter ends, large double or triple windows, exterior chimneys and large gabled porches with conspicuous posts. What makes these posts notable is their two-part design. Although variations exist, the typical bungalow porch post consists of a tapered or straight column rising from a thick supporting pier. Paired columns atop single piers are also common. Important interior features include paneled rooms with beamed ceilings and fireplaces as well as casual, hall-less floorplans. Between 1910 and 1930 whole suburbs of bungalows appeared on the landscape. Baton Rouge's Roseland Terrace subdivision (1911) is an excellent example.

Although America made the bungalow its own, the first buildings to be known as bungalows appeared in India when the colonial government adapted the typical low, galleried native hut into a series of rest houses for British travelers. Bengali natives called the houses *banglas,* while in the Hindu language *bangla* meant "belonging to Bengal." Britishers corrupted these like-sounding words to serve as the structures' name.[1] Returning soldiers and diplomats then carried the idea of the low-slung bungalow to England, from where it migrated to the United States.

The first American bungalows were built as vacation houses for the wealthy. Nevertheless, intellectuals and progressive reformers soon focused upon the bungalow as the answer to the problems of noise, pollution, and crowding generated by the industrial age. Three separate yet related reform philosophies contributed

A classic bungalow in Baton Rouge's Roseland Terrace Subdivision.
Photo by Donna Fricker.

A shotgun in the bungalow style, Carrollton Historic District, New Orleans.
Photo by Donna Fricker.

A camelback bungalow in Baton Rouge.
Photo by Donna Fricker.

to the bungalow's evolution as a refuge for the middle-class worker. They were the back-to-nature craze, the progressive housing crusade, and the Arts and Crafts Movement.

Proponents of the back-to-nature philosophy believed that houses should be designed to take advantage of the simple pleasures and soothing quiet of nature. This meant that landscapes should be informal and romantic, while houses should provide easy access between indoor and outdoor spaces.[2] Progressive housing reformers strove to simplify the home's interior. It was this group which so opposed the formal Victorian home supposedly full of dusty, germ-laden surfaces. They proposed a natural, unpretentious, sanitary and efficient standardized house with a simple, compact and open plan. Sleeping porches for access to fresh air and small kitchens loaded with modern technological conveniences were additional characteristics of the progressive house.[3]

The Arts and Crafts Movement also sought to simplify the home. It arose from a fear that the machine age, with its accompanying availability of mass-produced goods, would create a materialistic consumer society capable of undermining America's morals. Therefore, Arts and Crafts proponents recommended that homebuilders eliminate fake ornament, use inexpensive but durable natural materials with natural finishes, paint exterior surfaces in colors harmonizing with the landscape, plan room placement according to function, and provide plenty of open space inside the home. Finally, Arts and Crafts proponents emphasized the promotion of craftsmanship itself.[4]

All of these proposals for housing reform coalesced in turn-of-the-century California. This western state was ripe for architectural experimentation because its mild climate and relaxed rural lifestyle had made it a mecca for Americans. The new arrivals, of course, needed affordable and quickly built houses. Although strongly influenced by the three reform philosophies, architects also drew upon American precedents to create the new "small" house which came to be known as the bungalow. For example, New England's colonial homes contributed the bungalow's emphasis upon the fireplace as a symbol of home and family, the Victorian Stick Style influenced the bungalow's emphasis on rusticity, and the mid-nineteenth-century writings of horticulturalist Andrew Jackson Downing popularized the use of natural materials and earth-toned colors which the bungalow adopted. The South is credited with influencing the bungalow's emphasis on the porch through the broad galleries associated with Louisiana's French Creole houses.[5] Two foreign architectural trends also contributed. Both the Swiss Chalet and the timber structures of Japan shared the Arts and Crafts philosophies of pride in craftsmanship and the use of natural materials such as wood.

A raised bungalow in the Mid-City Historic District, New Orleans.
Photo by Donna Fricker.

Around 1907, California architects Charles and Henry Greene became two of the first designers to combine the new ideas with the older stylistic precedents. Although the homes they designed are considered mansions today, they were called bungalows at the time. Soon their ideas trickled down to middle-class homes and the bungalow craze was on. Spread by numerous magazine articles, mail-order pattern books, and the availability of pre-fabricated houses, the bungalow quickly moved beyond California to the rest of the nation. Soon a variety of exterior stylistic variations developed, but all retained the basic features which made a house a bungalow.

For the most part, Louisiana's bungalows resemble those built throughout the United States. However, some regional interpretations did develop. Interestingly, these differences sometimes contradicted the bungalow's underlying philosophy. For example, the bungalow's distinctive column-atop-pier, gabled porch, and overhanging eaves were so popular that they were soon applied to other types of houses. This tendency led to a whole generation of single- and double-shotgun houses with bungalow details, built principally in New Orleans. However, true bungalows had open and flexible floorplans rather than the linear plan found in shotguns, and the bungalow was meant to serve as a single family home rather than a duplex.

Another Louisiana bungalow adaptation was also related to the shotgun. This development was the camelback—a house in which a partial second story rises above the first floor at the home's approximate mid-point. Camelback stories were originally a ploy for gaining more space within a shotgun, and the device was later applied to the bungalow. However, bungalows by definition were low, one- or one-and-one-half-story residences; so the camelback bungalow was also a significant deviation from the norm.

An additional Louisiana adaptation was the raised bungalow, which is basically a bungalow raised a full story on a high basement. The principal (upper) floor is usually reached by a prominent flight of stairs. Generally, the lower (basement) story is used for storage and service spaces. Larger than the single story variety, the raised bungalow was also more expensive to build. Thus, it contradicted the bungalow's avowed purpose of providing simple cost-effective housing for the masses. Although occasionally found elsewhere in Louisiana, the raised bungalow is essentially a New Orleans phenomenon.

The bungalow in its various forms dominated the American housing industry until the late 1920s. However, its very popularity contributed to its eventual decline. Cheap pattern-book copies eroded the public's confidence in the bungalow as an example of fine but affordable craftsmanship. At the same time, the social values which inspired the bungalow lost favor. Finally, the advent of the Depression blasted the construction business. After economic recovery and World War II, the housing industry turned toward other types and styles of residences. However, many Louisiana families live in bungalows today and their popularity is experiencing a rejuvenation as additional preservation-minded families discover their charms. It is hoped this trend will continue.

The Hispanic Revival

by Jonathan Fricker

The post-World War I era in America was a period of "flivvers," burgeoning suburbs, booming optimism, and speculation. Everyone it seemed wanted something "up-to-date." But the prevailing taste in architecture was anything but "up-to-date." Modern efficient homes and buildings were generally dressed in appropriate romantic period garb. Historic styles of architecture were not only beautiful in their own right, but came with a panoply of rich historical associations most cultured people could easily understand. Colonial was always appropriate for a small to medium size building, especially in the eastern states, be it a home, a church, or a county courthouse. If it was not Colonial, a church might be Gothic to bespeak our Christian heritage. Gothic might also be used for schools and colleges because it seemed to hearken back to the hallowed halls of Oxford and Cambridge. As architectural historian Walter Kidney has described it, a movie palace might be "something utterly fantastic . . . some sort of high pressure Mediterranean Baroque."[1] Buildings erected in the southwestern United States might feature a Latin style such as Mission or Spanish Colonial.

In some ways the art and architecture world was admitting defeat. While the nineteenth century had struggled on and off to evolve a style of its own appropriate to "modern" times, many now believed that the concept of architecture was settled once and for all. As society interior decorator Elsie de Wolfe, "the chintz lady," wrote during these years: "We cannot do better than to accept the standards of other times, and adapt them to our own uses."[2] It was regrettable, she felt, but true.

A rising generation of architects, either trained or influenced by the French École des Beaux Arts, could produce a convincing design in just about any style from any period, whatever the client wanted. Moreover, architectural features ranging from terra-cotta columns to cast-stone arches to cast-plaster cornices were manufactured all over the country and could be easily shipped by rail to the building site.

The practice of designing "in the period" was both described and satirized in 1945 in a small book called *Tomorrow's House.* In it a "great" architect receives a

An old postcard view of the Colorado Southern Depot in Crowley (1907). The building has since lost the top stage of its tower. Courtesy of the Division of Historic Preservation.

Harahan Elementary School (1926), William R. Burk, Architect. Photo by Donna Fricker.

Harahan Elementary School
Photo by Donna Fricker.

commission for a new house. "Gratified, the Great Architect smiled benignly and reached behind him for the well-thumbed copies of *Stately Homes of the English Aristocracy of the Eighteenth Century* by Marmaduke Chilblane . . . and *Rooms Louis XIV Was Particularly Fond Of* by Lady Meddle. The Great Architect was ready to design another house."[3]

As Walter Kidney has pointed out, architects who practiced the period look were not ideological or intellectual. They merely wanted to create a pleasant experience.[4] This, of course, was in sharp contrast to the fiercely dogmatic glass-box modernist movement that was to follow.

Velva Street Fire Station (1924), Shreveport. Photo courtesy of Noel Memorial Library, Archives and Special Collections, Louisiana State University-Shreveport.

Of the many "period looks" popular between the two world wars, the two most in evidence in Louisiana are interpretations of Hispanic and English architecture. The broad Hispanic Revival category includes the Mission Revival, the Spanish Colonial style, and a sort of adobe Pueblo Revival native to New Mexico. Of these, the first two are found in Louisiana.

Neo-Hispanic architecture was and is rather poorly defined. One critic of the period perhaps best described it as the "Bastard-Spanish-Moorish-Romanesque-Gothic-Renaissance-Bull Market-Damn-the-Expense" style of architecture.[5] And while it had its excesses, the Hispanic mode did produce a convincing, easily

A. C. Steere Elementary School, Shreveport, 1929, Edward F. Neild, Architect. Photo by Donna Fricker.

recognizable archetype which has added much to the character of our cities and towns.

It was in California, Rexford Newcomb's "true daughter of old Spain," that the Hispanic architectural revival began.[6] In many ways it is seen as a western response to the Colonial Revival in the eastern states, and not a friendly one at that. In 1882 a group of California aesthetes, led by San Francisco designer Harold Mitchell, launched an appeal for a "genuinely native architecture" appropriate to the golden west. In the ensuing years eastern architecture became increasingly disparaged as out of place amid the "glare, newness and rush of western life." The white-painted boxes of the Colonial Revival were particularly lampooned. "Puritan" dwellings they were called, "so white and bloodless as to be strongly suggestive of a prolonged cold-water diet."[7]

Increasingly, westerners turned to the Franciscan missions of old California as a source of inspiration for new buildings. Much of the credit for this revival belongs to Charles Fletcher Lummis, a vigorous promoter and chauvinistic editor of the *Land of Sunshine.* Lummis used the magazine to popularize Spanish culture, folk songs, art, and architecture. He was ultimately knighted by the Spanish government for his efforts. Lummis wrote that the Franciscan missions "are worth more than money" and "a man is a poor fool who thinks he can do business without sentiment." The latter quality was much in evidence in a series of articles Lummis ran in the mid-1890s arguing the suitability of old Spanish buildings as the true basis for a native architecture of the West.[8] Mission-inspired buildings began to appear in goodly numbers as the twentieth century dawned.

One of the factors that spread the popularity of the Mission Revival was the decision by various southwestern-based railroad companies to build their depots and hotels in the Mission style. A good example of this is a depot built in Crowley, Louisiana, by the Colorado Southern Railroad in 1907. Thought to be Louisiana's earliest full-fledged Hispanic Revival building, the Crowley depot features several standard California mission elements. It has a rather massive feeling with white stucco walls suggesting adobe (mud brick) construction. The roof is low, hip, and

There are several surviving Mission Revival gas stations in Louisiana. This well preserved, classic small town example is on Main Street in Jeanerette. Photo by Donna Fricker.

The Spanish hacienda look in the Monroe Garden District. Photo by Donna Fricker.

One of several Spanish-looking houses near the fairgrounds in New Orleans. Note the tile roof, rough plaster, shaped gable, and arched openings. Photo by Donna Fricker.

spreading with four curving Baroque gables. The depot culminates in a central ecclesiastical-looking tower with a double-arched belfry under a pyramid-shaped roof. Like most mission-inspired buildings, the Crowley depot has little in the way of decorative ornament. Adobe, the original mission building material, was at best hard to sculpt.

Soon the Mission style was joined by the Spanish Colonial Revival, a more richly ornamental style based upon Mexican Baroque architecture. Spanish Colonial had an early and convincing show of power in the 1915 Panama-California Exposition held in San Francisco to celebrate the opening of the Panama Canal. Its popularity blossomed in the 1920s and 1930s with examples appearing in all parts of the country. Like the Mission style, Spanish Colonial architecture favored substantial white stucco walls, overhanging red-tile roofs, arched openings and towers. But while the Mission style generally eschewed ornament, the Spanish Colonial indulged in it richly, sometimes shamelessly. Windows were frequently covered with decorative grilles called *rejas*, which were either wrought iron or composed of turned wooden columns. Doors and windows were plied with a rich elaboration of motifs ranging from scrolls to cartouches to multiple superimposed colonnettes. A popular device was to substitute twisted Persian columns for ordinary porch posts. In asymmetrical examples ornament was often varied from opening to opening, creating a rich and interesting effect.

Louisiana's greatest concentration of high-style Spanish Colonial buildings is in Jefferson Parish. Conspicuous among this group is the 1926 Harahan Elementary School designed by William R. Burk. The building culminates in a two-story domed entrance rotunda with a Moorish-looking tile floor and a graceful curving stair and balcony of cast steel designed to resemble old Spanish wrought iron. The facade of the rotunda is a writhing sea of architecture and ornament, with richly molded curving Baroque openings, Persian columns and a vast panoply of multiple superimposed forms. It gives the eye little rest. Other high-style examples in the parish are St. Joseph Church in old Gretna and the Hope Haven and Madonna Manor complexes in Marrero.

But full-fledged Spanish Colonial buildings like those in Jefferson Parish are rare in Louisiana. The general trend of the period was for Mission and Spanish Colonial architecture to merge into a generic Hispanic look, with white plaster walls, low red-tile roofs and some ornament. This, of course, was also the general trend for the nation as a whole.

An interesting example of this hacienda look is the Velva Street Fire Station constructed in Shreveport in 1924. Here the desire for the romance of the Southwest was so strong that in its day the building even had a cactus garden. Additional romance is derived from the stucco which is applied deliberately in a rough and irregular manner. The fire-engine doorway is capped by a sinuous Baroque-shaped gable inset with a crest, a feature that lends a stately air to what might otherwise be considered a rustic rancho. All in all, the Velva Street Fire Station has that combination of formal and informal elements that distinguishes many Hispanic Revival buildings in Louisiana.

Hispanic Revival buildings of this kind are romantic and evocative rather than archaeologically correct. Indeed, many borrow from several periods of Spanish architecture without being heavily indebted to any of them—an archway here, a Persian column there, or over there a wobbly adobe-looking wall.

Louisiana's collection of Hispanic Revival buildings is mainly in large metropolitan areas such as Shreveport and New Orleans. There are also a few surviving depots and a modest scattering of stucco, tile-roofed filling stations. In regard to the latter, a "watered down" Spanish style seems to have been a particular favorite with Texaco.

The heyday of Spanish Revival architecture in Louisiana was the 1920s and 1930s, although examples continued to be built after World War II. It represents a type of architecture not native to the Pelican State, unless one considers that like California, Louisiana was once a part of the Spanish colonial empire. However, this may be stretching things a bit. On the whole, the style took root here largely because of its nationwide popularity. And although we have fewer and less elaborate examples than places like California or Texas, our neighborhoods would be much the poorer without them.

The English Styles

by Donna Fricker

Like the rest of the country, Louisianians often looked to the past for architectural inspiration in the 1920s and 1930s. It was a period in American architecture when long-ago and faraway styles captured public imagination. Our cities and suburbs were replete with French chateaux, Spanish-looking churches, Mediterranean villas, and quaint "olde English" cottages. As an ad for a "Norman French farmhouse" proclaimed: "Enter here . . . and leave the commonplace world outside!"[1]

Probably the most popular source of design inspiration was England—specifically, English architecture of the late medieval, Elizabethan and Jacobean periods (fifteenth, sixteenth and early seventeenth centuries). This Anglophilia took various forms. Domestic English Revival architecture ran the gamut from grand architect-designed Tudor or Jacobean mansions that closely resemble great English country houses to very simple cottages that someone from the Mother Country would not recognize. There was also a new generation of English Gothic churches. Educational institutions often took their cue from Oxford and Cambridge, creating a style known as "Collegiate Gothic." If schools were not reminiscent of "Oxbridge," they might resemble a Jacobean country house.

The picturesque English look was wildly popular for residences, whether they be baronial halls or cozy cottages. At the upmarket end were the so-called "Stockbroker Tudor" houses, a name used at the time because of the type's popularity with Wall Street financiers for country retreats. In atypical cases, architects actually traveled to England to study examples firsthand for their wealthy clients.

For middle-class America, the style was popularized through mail-order house catalogs such as Sears and Montgomery Ward and magazines such as *House Beautiful* and *House and Garden*. In some ways the tract houses of their day, the various models were advertised with evocative names such as "The Devonshire," "The Sussex," "The Hathaway," and "The Dover."[2]

The advertisements labeled the models as "old English" and "Quaint English Style Cottage." Some copy extolled the virtues of "the cottage homes of England"

An impressive "Stockbroker Tudor" house in Shreveport's Fairfield Historic District. Photo by Donna Fricker.

An example of the English cottage look in Roseland Terrace Historic District, Baton Rouge. Note the steeply pitched main gable and entrance gable and the prominent front chimney. Photo by Donna Fricker.

The Jacobean Revival Ouachita Parish High School, Monroe, 1924, H. H. Land, Architect.
Photo by Donna Fricker.

with their appearance of "solid comfort," while the ad for "The Devonshire" (costing $2,396) pictured flappers taking tea on the covered side porch.[3]

Architectural historians have termed these English cottages, as well as the upmarket versions, "Tudor Revival." Like the Queen Anne Revival, this is a misnomer. The style in question is eclectic, borrowing loosely from Tudor, Elizabethan and Jacobean architecture. In its watered down builder's form the origins are sometimes barely recognizable.

Regardless of what you call them, so-called Tudor Revival houses share certain readily identifiable characteristics, whether owned by John Doe or a Rockefeller. First and foremost is picturesque massing created by multiple steeply pitched gables. Often the facade is dominated by a steeply pitched gable and a smaller entrance gable. Decorative multi-flue chimneys with chimney pots enhance the picturesque massing. Typically, a chimney is located prominently on the facade. The front doorway is often arched and outlined with contrasting materials in an exaggerated fashion. Windows, in imitation of "olde English" examples, sometimes have diamond-pattern leaded glass or an imitation thereof.

Perhaps the feature most closely associated with the "olde English" look in the public imagination is half-timbering, although it certainly does not have to be present to make a house Tudor Revival. A popular method of construction in medieval and post-medieval England, half-timbering consisted of heavy, irregularly placed exposed timbers with plaster infill. In the American Tudor Revival, the wooden members were decorative rather than structural. In some examples, the beams were deliberately chopped with an ax to give the place that authentically ancient look. Montgomery Ward noted in its catalog that dark brown stain would be provided for such trim unless notified otherwise.[4]

There are countless examples of Tudor Revival houses in Louisiana, with the grandest and most high style being in large metropolitan areas such as New Orleans, Baton Rouge and Shreveport. Even small communities often have one or two examples of the builder's version of the English cottage look.

Another place to look for the English influence is in our educational institutions. A very select few in Louisiana are in the Jacobean Revival style, taking their cue from the great Jacobean country houses built in England in the early seventeenth century. The most noticeable feature of the standard Jacobean Revival school is the use of curved gables crowned by spiky, obelisk-like finials. Typically, various projections are outlined with quoins in a contrasting material. The style often makes extensive use of strapwork—interlocking decorative bands popular in Elizabethan and Jacobean England. These as well as other features can best be seen in Louisiana's two finest examples of the style—Ouachita Parish High School in Monroe and Byrd High in Shreveport. Other noteworthy examples are on the Northwestern State University campus in Natchitoches.

More popular for schools was the Collegiate Gothic style. Certain historic styles just seemed more appropriate for certain types of buildings, with the Gothic

Marquette Hall, Loyola University, New Orleans, 1910, de Buys, Churchill and Labouisse, Architects. Photo by Donna Fricker.

The Collegiate Gothic Baton Rouge High School, 1926,
William T. Nolan, Architect. Photo by Donna Fricker.

Above and left: Gothic detailing, Baton Rouge High School. Photos by Donna Fricker.

A new generation of English Gothic churches was built in the 1920s. Shown here is the First Presbyterian Church in downtown Baton Rouge. Photo by Donna Fricker.

buildings of Oxford and Cambridge being an obvious source of inspiration for educational institutions. A too-good-to-be-true story has it that one American university wrote to Oxford officials for advice on how to build a Gothic chemistry laboratory. "We cannot help you," replied the chemists at Oxford. "We haven't built a Gothic building for four hundred years."[5]

What has come to be known as Collegiate Gothic was introduced at Bryn Mawr and Princeton in the 1890s. It soon became quite fashionable for any self-respecting university, with Yale, Duke and the University of Chicago jumping on the bandwagon. Sometimes the enthusiasm for Gothic and instant antiquity got out of control in the hands of over-enthusiastic architects. For example, James Gamble Rogers tried to "early up" his Yale designs by wearing down the steps with grinding wheels to suggest centuries of use.[6]

The Collegiate Gothic style ranges from fully developed high-style designs resembling their English prototypes to buildings whose "Gothicness" is not as intensive, often resting on applied ornamentation. A good example of the former is Loyola University in New Orleans. Particularly noteworthy is the massing of the main building, Marquette Hall, which culminates in a central pavilion framed by barbican-like towers. A great entrance archway flanked by octagonal towers was all the rage for castle building in England during the time of Henry VIII. Towers were originally necessary for defensive purposes, but by the quieter early sixteenth century, they had acquired associations with power and lordship. Thus, they were liberally used to ornament gentlemen's residences. Other noteworthy features at Marquette Hall are crenelation (the indentations along the top of the building) and smaller "towers" defining the edges.

A good example of a fairly standard school design made anything but standard by Gothic details is Baton Rouge High School. Located in a park-like setting along Government Street near downtown, the building has a typical five-part articulation—a projecting central portion with recessed wings and projecting end sections. Its overwhelming Gothic character is derived more from applied ornamentation than massing. Concentrated on the central pavilion, the copious terracotta detailing includes tracery and various types of foils (designs called trefoil, quatrefoil, etc. depending upon the number of arcs). A great lancet arch defines the entrance, above which is written "High School" in Gothic script. A dead giveaway to the school's less than English pedigree is the prominent bas-relief pelican at the top. What would an Oxford don make of that?

While some highbrows believe America's preoccupation with long-ago and faraway styles was the nadir of our architectural history, others are not quite so serious. Yes, imitation rather than originality was the order of the day, and yes, sometimes architects went to silly extremes. But oh how boring our landscape would be without the quaint English cottage here and there and fanciful school buildings evocative of another time and place. Romantic, yes, but infinitely preferable to the characterless houses and schools which blanket modern America.

Louisiana State Capitol, 1929, Weiss, Dreyfous & Seiferth, Architects.
Photo by Donna Fricker.

The Art Deco Style

by Jonathan Fricker

One of the most conspicuous products of the Jazz Age is what we now call Art Deco. In its day, it was termed "Modernistic." Spat upon by serious modernists,

The State Capitol is known for its rich sculptural ornamentation. Photo by Donna Fricker.

this manifestly urban style dazzled Depression Era America with frozen fountains, superimposed blossoms, symmetrically leaping impalas, and stylized human figures. Louisiana partook of this intoxicating style moderately, producing perhaps forty major examples, the best known being Huey Long's skyscraper State Capitol (1929-32).

Easy to recognize but difficult to define, Art Deco was an aggressively modern style inspired by various cultural sources. It was also the last universal style in that it embraced everything from cigarette lighters to cocktail cabinets to skyscrapers.

In many ways the style has its origins in the Cubist paintings of Pablo Picasso and his circle, and more specifically, in Futurism, which emerged in Italy in the early twentieth century. Called "a style in motion," Futurism embraced the philosophy that art must respond to the force and dynamism of modern life. Futurist works broke down human figures and other forms into repeating abstract geometric shapes suggesting force and movement. This repeating geometry is a fundamental ingredient in what would become the Art Deco style.[1]

Another source of inspiration was Mexico—Aldous Huxley's "Land of Your Golden Dream." In the 1920s and 1930s intellectuals became fascinated with the primitive cultures of the Aztecs and other Indian peoples of the Americas. Numerous books appeared showing geometric designs of the Zunis and Mayans, as well as the stepped pyramids of the Aztecs. The stepped pyramid was particularly important, giving its shape to many an Art Deco bookend set, sideboard and cutaway massed building.[2]

Scholars have also pointed to lesser influences on Art Deco such as Egyptian art, with its stylized human figures, popularized by the 1922 discovery of King Tutankhamen's tomb. Others have noted the influence of stage sets used in the Russian Ballet.[3]

These influences coalesced to form a very distinctive, energetic and exuberant style. It befitted its times. As British historian Bevis Hillier has pointed out, it was the day of the "Bright Young Things." "A generation starved of superfluity did not relish stark cubist paintings or the 'purism' of Ozenfant. They wanted colour, fizz and bubble."[4]

This new style had its first major showing in the 1925 *Exposition des Arts Decoratifs* held in Paris, which gave it worldwide attention. As noted earlier, the style was known in its day as "modernistic." The popular term "Art Deco" seems to date from the 1960s. Indeed, the catalog for a 1966 commemorative exhibition on the original 1925 show bore "Art Deco" as the subtitle. By the late 1960s the term appears to have been in general use.[5]

"Modernistic" architecture took root in America during the late 1920s. In Louisiana Huey Long adopted the style as an icon of the modern era and as a symbol of his bringing the state into the twentieth century. Long positively glowed with enthusiasm whenever he talked about his building projects and never more so than when he spoke of his plans for a new Louisiana capitol. In his efforts to convince the legislature that a new statehouse was needed, Long emphasized that an efficient modern capitol would actually save money. Trouble was, the new building was anything but efficient. Much of the first floor was taken up by a huge memorial hall with no specific function. Worse, the tall tower was too slender to provide much office space on each floor. And much of the space that was provided was taken up either by elevator shafts or stylish Art Deco setbacks. Then there was the matter of the costly figure sculpture and extensive bronze and marble decoration.[6]

Long's true purpose, of course, was to create a monument, and he succeeded. But it was a monument not everyone wanted. Long's opponents argued that the present capitol building was adequate, and that a new statehouse would be an extravagance. Huey's younger brother Earl joined the opposition, professing to dislike the architectural design of the building and arguing that a skyscraper style capitol would look like a "farm silo."[7] In the end, however, Huey prevailed, and his monument to himself is considered to be among the finest Art Deco buildings in

Municipal Memorial Auditorium, Shreveport, 1929, Sam Wiener, Architect.
Photo by Donna Fricker.

Rear elevation, Municipal Memorial Auditorium.
Photo by Donna Fricker.

Left: Pre-construction drawing of the National American Bank Building, New Orleans, 1929, Moise Goldstein, Architect. Courtesy of The Historic New Orleans Collection, Museum/Research Center, Charles Franck Collection, Acc. No. 1979.325.294. Right: The crowning glory of the National American Bank Building. Photo by Donna Fricker.

the South.

One wonders if Long's impressive capitol had an influence upon Louisiana civic architecture of the period. For example, of the fourteen parish courthouses constructed between the onset of the Depression and World War II, thirteen were in the Art Deco style. These buildings, along with a host of schools, town halls, and other public buildings, represent an overall architectural flowering made possible largely by a massive infusion of federal money.

New Deal relief funds were distributed much more freely to Louisiana after the death of Long in 1935. While the Kingfish had been a relentless adversary of the Roosevelt administration, his successors swore allegiance. In return, Justice Department tax investigations against high-ranking Longites were dropped and federal funds began to flow to the Pelican State. This "deal" was referred to at the time as "the Second Louisiana Purchase."[8] Regardless of its parentage, the result-ing federal largess caused an Art Deco building boom that covered the state with stylized geometric shapes, setback building masses, streamlined eagles and peli-cans, and muscular sculpted figures hard at work performing ordinary tasks.

One of the state's finest buildings from the era is the Ruston High School. This 1939 beige brick and limestone building features both hallmarks of the Art Deco—dramatic massing and extensive, stylized (usually geometric) ornamentation. It culminates in a dynamic, boldly vertical, faceted tower rising a full story above the main roofline. Classroom windows are strikingly articulated with a visually ener-getic system of pilaster strips which extend above the parapet. The building's or-namentation includes vertical strips accented with chevrons, stylized chevron swags, and various other geometric shapes. Bathed in early morning light, the school looks like something out of a 1930s futuristic movie. Equally impressive are the Port Allen High School in West Baton Rouge Parish and Neville High in Monroe.

Certainly the state's most intensively ornamented Art Deco building is the 1929 Shreveport Municipal Auditorium. Today the building is best remembered as the home of a musical program called *The Louisiana Hayride*. It was from the stage of the *Hayride* that a young Memphis truck driver named Elvis Presley first attracted national attention. Indeed, groups from around the world still tour the building just to stand on the very boards where the "King" once stood.

Architecturally, the building is a *tour de force* in intricately worked brick and carved limestone. Architect Sam Wiener pulled out all the stops to create a surface in which the eye gets no rest. Unlike many architects of the period in Louisiana, who seldom strayed from convention, Sam Wiener and his brother William were highly original and creative.

Note, for example, the fly gallery on the rear elevation, an awkward tall feature required in all theaters which most architects left blank and hoped nobody would notice. But Wiener did just the opposite, exploiting the verticality of the fly gallery with four massive upward thrusting piers interspersed with recessed areas of richly decorative brickwork, making the gallery a dramatic climax for the rear elevation.

Major commercial examples of the Art Deco taste are rare in Louisiana. The National American Bank Building in New Orleans, 1929, is certainly the state's most impressive example. Its architect, Moise Goldstein, drew upon contempo-rary trends, using a system of ascending piers and setbacks which was a very popular and much admired way of articulating large skyscrapers during the 1920s and early 1930s. The technique was popularized in renderings by Hugh Ferriss showing cutaway ribbed masses dramatically bathed in light. This style represented the "state of the art" prior to the onset of the glass-box International Style. The climax of the National American Bank Building is an elaborate rooftop water tower which almost conjures up an image of a 1930s spaceship. It shows why Art Deco is some-times irreverently called the "Flash Gordon" style of architecture.

Ruston High School, 1939, J. W. Smith & Associates, Architects.
Photo by Donna Fricker.

Art Deco residences are rare in Louisiana, as indeed they are in the rest of the
country. Art Deco's urbane, vigorously geometric and futuristic feeling did not
provide the kind of cozy cottage image most suburbanites wanted to come home

to. According to art historian Russell Lynes, this feeling was shared by realtors and bank loan officers. After all, he wrote, "Suppose a man built a Modern house and then moved away, who would take it over?"[9]

Of the few Art Deco residences built in Louisiana, the Rankin mansion in St. Tammany Parish is certainly the most impressive. Unfinished until recently, and with its architect unknown, this 1939 Modernistic villa commands a beautiful wooded site on Cane Bayou. Construction stopped abruptly when its owner, State Conservation Commissioner William Rankin, became embroiled in the notorious political scandals of 1939. Abandoned for many years, the house was renovated within the last few years by Justin Wilson for use in his cooking shows, a happy end to the story.

These and other buildings constitute Louisiana's Art Deco legacy. Because they are recent, they are apt to be under appreciated. Indeed, many remember a time before they were built. Nonetheless, they represent a distinct era in the history of taste, an era closed and gone for fifty years, and an exciting era, especially compared to the architectural pablum that was to follow. Most of these buildings are well preserved, a testament to the farsightedness and sensitivity of their owners.

Rankin House, St. Tammany Parish, 1939.
Photo by Donna Fricker.

Endnotes

Chapter One: The French Creole Style

[1]Telephone interview with Jay D. Edwards, Louisiana State University Department of Geography and Anthropology, January 30, 1997.

[2]For a discussion on the possible sources of Creole architecture see Jay D. Edwards, *Louisiana's Remarkable French Vernacular Architecture, 1700-1900.* First Monograph of the Fred B. Kniffen Cultural Resources Laboratory (Baton Rouge, La., 1988), 2-10 and Jonathan Fricker, "Origins of the Creole Raised Plantation House," *Louisiana History,* 25 (1984): 137-53.

[3]Edwards, *Louisiana's Remarkable French Vernacular Architecture,* 8.

[4]Stephen Hand, "The Development of French Quarter Courtyards and French Quarter Style," Paper delivered at the New Orleans Architecture Symposium, New Orleans, November 2, 1991, paraphrased in Jay D. Edwards, "Cultural Identifications in Architecture: The Case of the New Orleans Townhouse," *Traditional Dwellings and Settlements Review: Journal of the International Association for the Study of Traditional Environments,* 5 (1993): 27.

[5]Samuel Wilson, Jr., *The Architecture of Colonial Louisiana: Collected Essays of Samuel Wilson, Jr., F.A.I.A.,* Jean M. Farnsworth and Ann M. Masson, compilers and editors (Lafayette, La., 1987), 333; and Edwards, "Cultural Identifications," 23-24, 30.

[6]Edwards, "Cultural Identifications," 28.

Chapter Two: The Greek Revival Style

[1]Russell Lynes, *The Tastemakers: The Shaping of American Popular Taste* (New York, 1980), 24.

[2]John Summerson, *Architecture in Britain, 1530-1830* (New York, 1983), 413; John Fleming, Hugh Honour and Nikolaus Pevsner, *The Penguin Dictionary of Architecture* (Harmondsworth, Middlesex, England, 1972), 125.

[3] For a general account of Greek and Gothic architecture in England during this period, see John Summerson, *Architecture in Britain*, 509-36.

[4]John Maass, *The Gingerbread Age: A View of Victorian America* (New York, 1957), 32.

[5]Ibid., 34; Lynes, *Tastemakers*, 13.

[6]Alexander O. Boulton, "From the Greek," *American Heritage* (November 1990): 81.

Chapter Three: The Gothic Revival Style

[1]Mark Twain, *Life on the Mississippi* (New York, 1917), 332-33.

[2]Calder Loth and Julius Trousdale Sadler, Jr., *The Only Proper Style: Gothic Architecture in America* (Boston, 1975), 82.

[3]Loth and Sadler, *Only Proper Style*, 11-12. For general background, see also Kenneth Clark, *The Gothic Revival: An Essay in the History of Taste* (New York, 1962), 46-65.

[4]Clark, *Gothic Revival*, 122; Loth and Sadler, *Only Proper Style*, 57-58; Phoebe B. Stanton, *The Gothic Revival & American Church Architecture: An Episode in Taste, 1840-1856* (Baltimore, 1968), 9, 15.

[5]Loth and Sadler, *Only Proper Style*, 60; Stanton, *Gothic Revival*, 3-29.

[6]Mills Lane, *Architecture of the Old South: Louisiana* (New York, 1990), 143, 149, 157, 160, 161, 163.

[7]Russell Lynes, *The Tastemakers: The Shaping of American Popular Taste* (New York, 1980), 24.

Chapter Four: The Italianate Style

[1]Andrew Jackson Downing, *Cottage Residences, Rural Architecture and Landscape*

Gardening (n.p., 1967), 22.

[2]Joan G. Caldwell, "Italianate Domestic Architecture in New Orleans, 1850-1880" (Ph. D. dissertation, Tulane University, 1975), 48-60.

[3]Ibid., 51.

[4]Ibid., 51, 55-56.

[5]Ibid., 71.

[6]Ibid., 65.

[7]Ibid., 78.

[8]John Maass, *The Gingerbread Age: A View of Victorian America* (New York, 1957), 11.

[9]Ann M. Masson and Lydia J. Owen, *Cast Iron and the Crescent City* (New Orleans, 1975), 46-47.

[10]Maass, *Gingerbread Age*, 99.

Chapter Five: The Eastlake Style

[1]Russell Lynes, *The Tastemakers: The Shaping of American Popular Taste* (New York, 1980), 101, 103.

[2]Charles L. Eastlake, *Hints on Household Taste* (New York, 1969). See, for example, pages 60, 65, 75, 213 and Plates XXI and XXIV.

[3]Lynes, *Tastemakers*, 100.

[4]Ibid., 101.

[5]Ibid., 105.

[6]Eastlake, *Hints on Household Taste*, xxiv; Marcus Whiffen, *American Architecture Since 1780: A Guide to the Styles* (Cambridge, Mass., 1969), 124.

[7]Whiffen, *American Architecture Since 1780,* 124.

[8]Lynes, *Tastemakers*, 101.

Chapter Six: The Queen Anne Revival Style

[1]Mark Girouard, *Sweetness and Light: The "Queen Anne" Movement, 1860-1900* (New Haven, 1977), 4.

[2]Russell Lynes, *The Tastemakers: The Shaping of American Popular Taste* (New York, 1980), 130.

[3]Girouard, *Sweetness and Light*, 90.

[4]Girouard, *Sweetness and Light*, 1; Lynes, *The Tastemakers*, 108.

[5]Walter C. Kidney, *The Architecture of Choice: Eclecticism in America, 1880-1930* (New York, 1974), 6.

[6]Mark Girouard, *The Victorian Country House: Revised and Enlarged Edition* (New Haven and London, 1979), 74.

[7]Marcus Whiffen, *American Architecture Since 1780: A Guide to the Styles* (Cambridge, Mass., 1969), 117-18.

Chapter Seven: The Colonial Revival Style

[1]Henry James, *Hawthorne* (New York and London, 1879), 12.

[2]James C. Massey and Shirley Maxwell, "Early Colonial Revival," *Old House Journal* (March/April 1990): 46, 48.

[3]Walter C. Kidney, *The Architecture of Choice: Eclecticism in America, 1880-1930* (New York, 1974), 32.

[4]Frank E. Wallis, "The Colonial Renaissance Houses of the Middle and Southern Colonies," *An Architectural Monograph on Houses of the Southern Colonies*, The White Pine Series, 2 (February 1916), 6.

[5]"Business Women Are to Dedicate New Club House," *Monroe Morning World*, October 27, 1929.

[6]Alvin Redman, ed., *The Wit and Humor of Oscar Wilde* (New York, 1959), 124.

Chapter Eight: The Beaux Arts and Neo-Classical Styles

[1]Marcus Whiffen, *American Architecture Since 1780: A Guide to the Styles* (Cambridge, Mass., 1969), 167.

[2] Marcus Whiffen and Frederick Koeper, *American Architecture, Volume 2: 1860-1976* (Cambridge, Mass., 1981), 268, 273-76; Frederick Platt, *America's Gilded Age: Its Architecture and Decoration* (South Brunswick and New York, 1976), 13-14. For additional background on the 1893 world's fair, see David F. Burg, *Chicago's White City of 1893* (Lexington, Ky., 1976).

[3]Platt, *America's Gilded Age*, 17.

[4]Russell Lynes, *The Tastemakers: The Shaping of American Popular Taste* (New York, 1980), 142.

[5]Walter C. Kidney, *The Architecture of Choice: Eclecticism in America, 1880-1930* (New York, 1974), 49.

Chapter Nine: The Bungalow Style

[1]Clay Lancaster, *The American Bungalow, 1880-1930* (New York, 1985), 19. For an overview of the bungalow's development worldwide, see Anthony D. King, *The Bungalow: The Production of a Global Culture* (London, 1984).

[2]Laura Chase, "Eden in the Orange Groves: Bungalows and Courtyard Houses of Los Angeles," *Landscape,* 25 (1981): 32; Clifford Edward Clark, Jr., *The American Family Home, 1880-1960* (Chapel Hill, N.C., 1986), 180. For an overview of the back to nature movement, see Peter J. Schmitt, *Back to Nature: The Arcadian Myth in Urban America* (New York, 1969).

[3]For an overview of the progressive housing movement, see Chapter 9 in Gwendolyn Wright, *Building the Dream: A Social History of Housing in America* (New York, 1981), 158-76.

[4]Clark, *American Family Home*, 181; H. Allen Brooks, "Chicago Architecture: Its

Debt to the Arts and Crafts," *Journal of the Society of Architectural Historians*, 30 (December 1971): 312-17; and Patricia Poore, "The Bungalow and Why We Love It So," *Old House Journal* (May 1985): 90. For a summary of the Arts and Crafts philosophy see Gustav Stickley, *More Craftsman Homes: Floor Plans and Illustrations for 78 Mission Style Dwellings* (New York, 1912; reprint ed., New York, 1982): 1-4; Paul Duchscherer, *The Bungalow: America's Arts and Crafts Home* (New York, 1995), 2-11.

[5]Lancaster, *American Bungalow*, 46-48.

Chapter Ten: The Hispanic Revival Styles

[1]Walter C. Kidney, *The Architecture of Choice: Eclecticism in America, 1880-1930* (New York, 1974), 2.

[2]Russell Lynes, *The Tastemakers: The Shaping of American Popular Taste* (New York, 1980), 185-86.

[3]George Nelson and Henry Wright, eds., *Tomorrow's House: How to Plan Your Post-War Home Now* (New York, 1945), 14.

[4]Kidney, *Architecture of Choice*, 1-4.

[5]W. A. Swanberg, *Citizen Hearst: A Biography of William Randolph Hearst* (New York, 1961), 367.

[6]Harold Kirker, *California's Architectural Frontier: Style and Tradition in the Nineteenth Century* (Santa Barbara, Calif., 1973), 125.

[7]Ibid., 120, 114-15.

[8]Ibid., 121-22.

Chapter Eleven: The English Styles

[1]Russell Lynes, *The Tastemakers: The Shaping of American Popular Taste* (New York, 1980), 238.

[2]Robert Schweitzer and Michael W. R. Davis, *America's Favorite Homes: Mail-Order Catalogues as a Guide to Popular Early 20th-Century Houses* (Detroit, 1990), 173-87.

[3]Ibid., 178-79, 181.

[4]Ibid., 176.

[5]Lynes, *Tastemakers*, 242.

[6]Walter C. Kidney, *The Architecture of Choice: Eclecticism in America, 1880-1930* (New York, 1974), 61.

Chapter Twelve: The Art Deco Style

[1]Bevis Hillier, *Art Deco of the 20s and 30s* (London, 1968; New York, 1985), 26-34.

[2]Ibid., 40-50.

[3]Ibid., 52-55, 35-39.

[4]Ibid., 61.

[5]Ibid., 11-12.

[6]Vincent F. Kubly, *The Louisiana Capitol: Its Art and Architecture* (Gretna, La., 1977), 15.

[7]T. Harry Williams, *Huey Long* (New York, 1970), 484-85.

[8]Allan P. Sindler, *Huey Long's Louisiana: State Politics, 1920-1952* (Baltimore, 1956), 86, 126-27.

[9]Russell Lynes, *The Tastemakers: The Shaping of American Popular Taste* (New York, 1980), 247.